Does
Theological Education
Make a Difference?

D1566079

Does
Theological Education
Make a Difference?

Global Lessons in
Mission and Ministry
from India and Britain

Andrew Wingate

WCC Publications *Geneva*

Cover design: Edwin Hassink

ISBN 2-8254-1320-8

© 1999 WCC Publications, World Council of Churches,
150 route de Ferney, 1211 Geneva 2, Switzerland
Web site: http://www.wcc-coe.org

No. 87 in the Risk Book Series

Printed in Switzerland

Table of Contents

Foreword

Andrew Wingate has graced the world of theological education and ministerial training with the fresh insights he offers in this significant book.

When Andrew went to South India to teach at Tamilnadu Theological Seminary (TTS), he was seen in traditional terms as a "missionary teacher". He reversed that tradition by simultaneously turning himself into a serious and engaging student, thus challenging the "teacher complex" of Western Christianity, from which churches in all parts of the world have yet to recover. When a "missionary" becomes a learner in this way, those who were formerly at the "receiving end" can build up the confidence to become "reciprocal missionaries" or partners in world mission. As one who is now in such a position in Britain, I am grateful, along with many of my fellow students and colleagues, for the encouragement and support provided by Andrew. Since leaving India, he has never allowed the transforming experience he gained there to remain a matter of the past. He has kept the links alive not simply by returning to visit occasionally but more significantly by arranging regular student exchanges and occasional staff exchanges, both between Queen's College and TTS, and between the United College of the Ascension and a number of churches and Christian institutions in India and other parts of the South. Such exchanges have not been a matter of sterile reciprocation, like the formal conventions of hospitality, but opportunities for continuing interaction of mutual learning and enrichment.

The institution presented in this book as a prime example of new patterns for theological education and ministerial training has been the longest home of my adult life, first as a TTS student, then as a staff member. When Andrew arrived there in 1975-76, I was in my final year as a student. Although training to be a minister like others, a special focus was attached to my formation, and that was mission. The Mission Institute operating within TTS was trying to give the dimension of mission to every aspect of theological training. There were many changes in the perspectives of some students, which were not without struggle. For some of us the outcome was – as a fellow student and colleague and I have put it in *Venturing into Life* (the story of the first 20 years of TTS) – nothing less than a "conversion from fundamentalism to the fundamentals of the Bible". This placed us between two extreme positions – continued loyalty to conservative and even fundamentalist trends characteristic of the sending churches on the one hand, and carefree liberalism on the other. Certainly there were challenges awaiting those of us who followed this "middle path". On completion of my training, I was invited to stay on in the seminary to take up a new ministry of interfaith dialogue, which has never been recognized by the mainstream churches in India. Responsibilities were added in the areas of teaching, of directing the lay theological education programme and of producing theological textbooks in Tamil. Andrew was an engaging and encouraging colleague in carrying out such responsibilities, and for a period, I also served as one of his successors in the ministry among the prisoners.

Andrew's practical experiences at TTS and his concurrent critical reflections provided fresh data for his research and writing. His earlier books on interfaith dialogue and religious conversion have reflected this very clearly. This present book can be seen as a climax in that series, with its fascinating presentation of the impact of the new ministerial training at TTS on the life and ministry of some former students. As a matter of fact, an initial impact study was launched in connection with the tenth anniversary celebrations of TTS, and I was directly involved in this study with Sam Amirtham, the first principal. For various reasons, this could not be continued; nor did a plan to revive and intensify it in connection with the Silver Jubilee celebrations materialize. By writing this book, Andrew has filled this gap, and one may hope that this study with its limited scope will stimulate a fuller study in the future.

The author has not confined this study to a single context and its challenges. The way he has interwoven into it his experience in the UK makes it more balanced and globally relevant. From the perspective of the rapidly changing patterns of theological education and ministerial training in Britain, this book can stimulate fresh thinking. While the need to break with the traditional patterns is unavoidable, there is widespread concern that the changes should not lead to a dilution of the depth, breadth and intensity of the education and training which have created some highly competent leaders, ministers and theologians with profound scholarship. Above all, the author's question about the purpose of theological education and ministerial training is very pertinent. He rightly observes that training should take into account that Britain is as much a "mission field" as South India. The point is not to perpetuate and justify a system but to motivate the churches to think of new forms of existence that can address emerging situations. For example, ecumenical initiatives in ministerial training in Britain are slow; and this can be frustrating for those, like the author, who have first-hand experience of the achievement in India in this area, best exemplified by TTS. If those trained for ministry are not motivated by an ecumenical vision and evangelistic passion which are integrally related, they will clearly be impotent to set up a counter-culture, which is the most urgent need of the hour in this country.

As those who have done reading in theological education know, this subject can be very dry and abstract. This book, however, represents a quite different style, characterized by actual stories and living encounters, with reflections and insights inbuilt. I have no doubt that it will stimulate thinking at the global level about relevant patterns of ministerial training. I thank my friend Andrew for this contribution and for asking me to write this foreword, and I commend this book to all who are committed to mission and ministry in a multi-religious milieu.

ISRAEL SELVANAYAGAM
Wesley College
Bristol, UK

1. A Personal Introduction

In the early 1970s, I studied for the ordained ministry in the Church of England. I received a good training which specialized in priestly formation. Lincoln Theological College (which sadly closed a few years ago) combined openness in theology and a strong liturgical tradition with an emphasis on pastoral ministry. It was a college that was not afraid of the word "liberal" in the best sense of that word. We learned much about the Bible, church history, doctrine and the craft of parish ministry. I am deeply grateful for this. But – though I was hardly aware of it at the time – we learned little of mission in its various forms, nor do I remember studying specifically the theology of mission. From the placements I had in parishes in the north of England, it was not yet obvious how steeply the church would decline in face of the rapid economic and social changes that would mark the first decade or so of our ministries. I also had placements in a prison and with an adoption agency. Here the emphasis was on pastoral practice rather than on social analysis or wider issues of mission.

As for world faiths, I went through my ministerial training oblivious to the fact that the majority of the world was not even nominally Christian. Islam never entered our horizons, and we talked of Judaism only as the religion of Jesus and Paul, not of living Jews as found in large numbers in several British cities. Not even the fact that my maternal grandfather was of German Jewish stock brought this home to me. This may have been a consequence of the reality that we thought little of the world church or of the Anglican Communion beyond the Church of England. Nor do I remember studying the history of "the mission field", as it was known then, even from a Eurocentric perspective.

Church history concentrated on the early fathers, the mediaeval period, the Reformation and British church history in the Victorian and 20th-century periods. A standard text was Owen Chadwick's monumental story of the Victorian church, in whose thousand or so pages matters outside England receive only a very peripheral mention. The ecumenical movement for us was a matter of talks about Anglican-Methodist unity in Britain, not about the Church of South India (CSI), the World Council of Churches or the beginnings of the liberation movements and the Programme to Combat Racism. My nearest contact with the wider world at Lincoln was my close friendship with a fellow student, the late Abraham Ayrookuzhiel, an Indian from Kerala, a great friend of M.M. Thomas and later assistant director of the Centre for the Study of Christianity and Society in Bangalore. It was Abraham who challenged me to consider working in India. "Come over and learn from us and share your ministry with us," he said.

First I had three years in a parish near Birmingham. South Asians were settling in the area, and I was disturbed by the racist rhetoric, joking and petty harassment around me. This was the heyday of the late Enoch Powell, an extremely able politician of the far right, who called eloquently and divisively for the repatriation of non-white settlers, warning that otherwise "rivers of blood" would flow in our cities. When I objected to such rhetoric, I was reminded that it was not *my* job which was threatened by "Pakis" (Pakistanis), nor would it be I who suffered if the value of the church house in which I was living was reduced by their moving to my street. "You do not live with them or work with them!" With the words of my friend Abraham echoing in my mind, I determined to go and "live with them and work with them". I applied to the Church Missionary Society for service in South India and was offered the choice of teaching in one of two seminaries. The one was described as being in a lush green land near the bluest of seas – in Kerala. The other was located in one of the dustiest, hottest and most crowded places in the world, full of Hindu temples – in Madurai, Tamilnadu. Knowing nothing of either, I sought the advice of Lesslie Newbigin.

His challenge left me little doubt about my choice. The veteran ecumenist and missionary described the Tamilnadu Theological Seminary (henceforth TTS) as potentially one of the most dynamic places of theological education in the world. Its principal was the visionary Sam Amirtham, later to work in Geneva as the director of the programme on theological education in the World Council of Churches, after which he became bishop of South Kerala. Amirtham had been called by Newbigin at a young age to form a united college for the Tamil churches, something he had dreamed of as early as the 1930s, as I have read in his unpublished diaries. In 1969 the Church of South India and the Lutheran churches established the seminary in Arasaradi, in a large Swedish mission compound, surrounded by slums, a couple of miles from the great Meenaakshi temple. Those responsible felt that it was a mission imperative to place the seminary in the heart of Tamil culture and the majority Hindu religion, rather than in the more Westernized colonial capital of Madras. A strong renewal of Tamil culture and language had been led by the Dravidian political movement DMK (Dravida Munnetra Kazhagam), which was concerned to maintain a very distinctive culture within the unity of the new India, recognizing the inevitable risk of being dominated by the majority Hindi-speaking belt in the North. Over the last 30 years the DMK or its offshoots has normally formed the state government in Tamilnadu, a state of more than 50 million people.

Madurai is a major centre of the cotton industry, where large numbers of hand-loom weavers try to compete with, or complement, the highly mechanized mills owned by multinational corporations. Though its population is over one million, it has in some ways much of the feel of village India. Into its many small communities and slums comes a daily influx of new residents from neighbouring districts, where agriculture depends on the vagaries of rainfall and heat and the majority remain landless or nearly so, seeking work.

Casteism is very strong in this southern part of India; and the Dalits (also known as Scheduled Castes or "untouchables"), who make up about 20 percent of the population, are often subjected to illegal bonded labour, which is *de facto* enslavement. Many women and children work for a pittance in factories that make matches or fireworks, in dangerous conditions that are a disgrace in any modern state. The other two main caste groupings are the priestly caste of Brahmins, who have traditionally held control, not least because this was useful for the British, and the Shudra "backward" castes, those just above the Dalits and most threatened by the government's efforts, through reverse discrimination, to uplift the Dalits.

Christians in this part of India are comparatively numerous – 5.78 percent in Tamilnadu, according to the 1981 census. The majority are Roman Catholic; and Madurai was the Indian home of the 18th-century pioneer of indigenous mission, Robert di Nobili. TTS serves mainly the seven Tamil dioceses of the Church of South India, the Tamil Evangelical Lutheran Church and the Arcot Lutheran Church. The majority of church members are rural and are Dalits, except in the two southern dioceses of Tirunelveli and Kanyakumari, where the Nadar community dominates (Nadars were associated with the tapping of Palmyra trees, a form of palm). Students from various parts of India come to TTS to study for a master's degree in theology; and ecumenical students come for short periods from all over the world.

I arrived in Tamilnadu with my wife and two young daughters at Epiphany in 1976. The Magi came from the east to find the stable, I went *to* the east and found the heart of my calling to ministry and mission and a strong sense of theological renewal. These have remained with me. It is with great gratitude, as well as with an analytical and reflective purpose, that I devote this book to considering the type of training available in this seminary and its consequences for those who become part of the church's ministry. As a teacher, I was deeply influenced by being at TTS. Thinking of the Bible in a radically different context from Europe affected me as I taught the New Testament, as I served as convenor of a prison ministry in the local jail, as I developed an internship programme, involving four-month student placements in challenging contexts throughout Tamilnadu and beyond, as I associated with various local congregations, as I engaged with people of other religions around the city. Above all, perhaps, I was affected by being part of the remarkable community of several hundred persons who made up the seminary and by being included in a faculty of theological teachers who saw their common purpose as transcending the particular subjects each happened to teach. The atmosphere could be summed up as: "If you have a good idea, whether you are a student or staff member, try it and evaluate it" – exactly opposite to the approach so often found: that you have to prove something from every angle before being given permission to take even a modest initiative.

Could the kind of transformation I had experienced also affect the students? To answer this question, I decided to study one particular class – the students who completed their training in 1982. I reflected with them individually on what they had learned in the previous four years, how they had learned and how they had been changed. When I discussed with them what they now considered to be the priorities for their future ministry, I was struck that most put some area of mission at the forefront of their thinking. I also asked what they thought might be the obstacles to achieving their hopes, within or outside of the church. Here they were appropriately realistic.

Since my return to England in 1982, I have made four further visits to Tamilnadu. I have met these same students individually, whether in their parish or the seminary, and have sought their reflections at each stage of their ministry, as well as talking with their parishioners and the church officials involved with them. The findings from these encounters form the centre of this book. As the title suggests, the central question I am trying to answer is whether theological education makes a difference. No matter how dynamic theological education may be, do external constraints – such as the conservatism of the local church and diocesan leaders, or the social and political realities of the context in which ministry is carried out – in practice prevent hopes from being fulfilled to any measurable extent? Or is it internal factors which predominate in moulding a ministry – so that a person generally reverts to what he or she was before coming into contact with the new approach introduced in the seminary? In this research, I was particularly interested in what was happening in mission – such spheres as inter-faith dialogue, evangelism, social work, working for social change and the indigenization of the church and its worship (itself a missionary task).

My aim is certainly not to judge any of the individuals in my study. The aim is rather to provide data for an evaluation of the deeper questions. In order to bring life to the study and enable readers from around the world to engage with it, a case study approach was taken. TTS is not a place without faults but it is a place that has been bold in innovation, hence its story is one worth sharing. It is a place that received much support from the Programme for Theological Education of the WCC, as well as from WCC churches in Europe and North America of the traditions which came together in the CSI – Anglican, Congregational, Reformed, Presbyterian, Methodist – and the Lutheran churches of Sweden, Germany and Denmark. These factors, as well as its special context, make it an ideal place to evaluate contextual theological education. At each stage in this study I have consulted with and been encouraged by the four principals of TTS; and the present principal, Dhyanchand Carr, has seen these pages. I have also been in regular contact with a number of faculty members, especially with Israel Selvanayagam, now at Wesley College, Bristol, who has read and commented on this manuscript and kindly agreed to contribute a foreword.

For continuity and comparison, I have taken a second example, the West Midlands Ministerial Training Course, based at the ecumenical Queen's Theological College, in Birmingham, England, and serving five Anglican dioceses in the centre of England and the Methodist and United Reformed churches. As principal here from 1982 until 1990, I was given a mandate to "contextualize" this course. Consciously at times, unconsciously at others, I used many of the insights I had gained in Tamilnadu, applying or adapting them to this very different context.

Like Tamilnadu, the Midlands area of England is a mixture of city, suburban and rural. But the former two contexts dominate, and unlike in India most villages are town-dependent. Compared with India, few people are directly involved in agriculture. India is industrializing rapidly; England, especially the Midlands, is well into the post-industrial era. The home of the Industrial Revolution has become an area where more people are involved in service industries than in production. The air in our cities is relatively clean, much different from those of India. Globalization certainly links both contexts, so that – to take one example – much more computer software is produced in India than in Britain.

The English Midlands has its own "Dalits", those left behind in the Thatcherite and "New Labour" Britain (though some attempts are now being made to reverse the income redistribution, which has been from the poor to the rich since 1979). These persons are found in the inner cities and on the outer-city estates. The area is also ethnically diverse. In Birmingham about one-third of births are to black or Asian citizens. Other places remain nearly all white. Religiously, Birmingham has more than a hundred places of Muslim worship, including what is said to be the largest mosque in Europe; it also has many places of Hindu, Sikh and Buddhist worship and a small but important Jewish community. The church has declined: no more than 5 percent of the population is actively part of any church, and fewer than 2 percent are in church on any one Sunday in the Church of England, the established church. While these figures are particularly low in Birmingham, there is no dramatic difference in other dioceses. The churches that are growing are black-led churches and house and Pentecostal churches, usually with a conservative theology.

It is within such a context that members of the West Midlands Course are called to minister. The number of students is between 40 and 60 at any one time, and they do their training for three years part-time. The basis of the course, as I helped to mould it, was that Britain is as much a "mission field" as South India and that ministerial training should take this into account.

Does theological education make a difference? I will address this question by looking in detail at the story of TTS (Chapter 2), at one of the projects I was involved in there

(Chapter 3), at the training and ministry of six particular students over twenty years (Chapter 4) and more generally (in Chapter 5) at the impact of TTS on the church as a whole. This is the major part of the book. For my second example I explain the model of training in Birmingham (Chapter 6) and consider seven students from that course who have now been in ministry for nearly ten years (Chapter 7). On this basis Chapter 8 addresses the question of how much difference theological education makes in both contexts.

Since 1990, I have come into contact with many other examples of theological education, both directly through visits to many countries and indirectly through students from around the world who have come to Selly Oak. While I might have added a good deal on the basis of this experience, this would risk overwhelming what is a comparatively short book and I have thus confined myself to these two examples – not because I think India and Britain are more important than other places, but because of my direct involvement and the way I have tried to make links between the two.

Readers are asked to consider the questions and the stories in relationship to what they know of theological training, ministry and mission in their own contexts. Each place has its own story – and that is one of the lessons demonstrated here. The goal is to enable the Christian gospel, itself both one and diverse, to interact with and challenge those different contexts. This happens through the church in each place and through the world in which the church is placed – where the working of God's Spirit may sometimes seem more obvious than it is within what we claim as "Christ's body". Theological education, whether for the ordained or for the laity, is one instrument for doing that. An enduring question is whether theological education is primarily to serve the church as it is, or is intended to challenge the church to be what it might be, as a sign of God's kingdom, but also an instrument of service, challenging and being challenged by the work of God's Spirit in the world.

2. The Training Experience at Tamilnadu

In 1970, after one year as the first principal of TTS, Samuel Amirtham wrote: "The only justification for a theological seminary of this size and quality in Tamilnadu is that it continually strives to make theology relevant and to preach the gospel effectively in Tamilnadu. Committed to the gospel of Jesus Christ, we believe we have the freedom in the Holy Spirit to experiment with new methods and to explore new frontiers. In this we need the blessings and understanding of the churches."

A crucial question for any seminary is its relationship with its sponsoring churches. For a seminary to ignore the churches is to make of itself an island. Crucial also is how faithful seminary alumni are to the vision they have caught as it becomes tested against the realities of everyday ministry. The bulk of this chapter will relate to the story of TTS until 1982, when the group of students I am researching graduated. To complete the story I will outline more briefly the main changes that have taken place since then. My main written source has been the seminary annual reports with appendixes on various aspects of the work. These numbered 24 by 1983. Beyond that I have drawn on my own experiences and my interviews with many faculty members.

Indigenization questions

As explained in the previous chapter, the choice of Arasaradi as the site for TTS was intentional. There was also a theological purpose behind the arrangement of the original buildings. The chapel was placed in the middle and was an open building so that a person walking to work or going to rest walks through the covered way in front of it, indicating that it is part of all life. Its design was adapted from local Dravidian (South Indian) temple architecture, and it is crowned with a *gopuram* (tower) which people of all faiths would associate with worship. At its top is a cross, leaving no doubts about in whose name the worship is offered. The inside, uncluttered and without chairs to allow liturgical experiment, is very light and airy, with open sides, down which vines later grew. A flood of light comes down from above, emphasizing Jesus Christ the light of the world.

The rest of the compound was designed by architect L. W. Baker as a series of small villages, with open space, fields and palm trees in between. Each "village" contains both family student and staff quarters and houses for domestic workers. This was done to make a statement about the inclusiveness of the community in the midst of a caste-ridden and hierarchical society. A feature of life as a result has been the way families – and in particular children – from different backgrounds have talked and played together.

In the first year after the seminary opened in 1969 certain focuses became clear. Besides training ordinands, TTS developed a strong sense of mission to the wider church. Seminars were held on indigenization of worship. Questions were soon raised about the limits to such indigenization, as the boundary with Hinduism becomes blurred. Even if something feels right in the seminary chapel, can it be passed on to the churches, for whom this whole subject is fraught with fear? TTS soon engaged someone to teach South Indian Carnatic music. How was this to be absorbed in a church whose more conservative elements considered the Western hymn, translated locally, as the most appropriate if not the only way to praise God?

From this initiative were developed much-loved Carnatic forms of worship, based on traditional Bhajan style, involving real participation for the congregation. Of the many songs written by students and staff, more than 100 were gathered into a songbook which became much used throughout the Tamil church. The words of the songs, both popular and classical, underscored the main theological priorities of the seminary: adherence to tradition, concern for indigenization, commitment to Christ and challenge to involvement in the world.

The seminary was also involved in a systematic attempt to change the style of Tamil language used in churches and in theological reflection. The Dravidian movement had brought a change to the language and worked especially to remove Sanskrit words, which were seen as Aryan. Two TTS staff members played a leading part in a new translation of the Bible, producing what became known as "Arasaradi Tamil". This attempted to bring to the Christian community the results of what was happening in the secular Tamil renaissance. Conservative Christians complained they could not understand such "high" Tamil. But it is significant that the Dravidian party chief minister opened the new student hostel at TTS; and a series of special lectures was held on such movements as the Dravidian movement, rationalism, communism, agnosticism and atheism.

More controversial was the commissioning of a series of bronzes on the life of Christ, crafted by a local Hindu artist named Chelladurai. Christ, Mary and others are portrayed in a style which is familiar because it is how Hindu gods and goddesses are pictured. While the artistic merit of this art was widely recognized, this was obscured by the sharp conflict which arose over the question of their legitimacy in a theological seminary. One diocese removed its students for a year, citing this among the problems. The bronzes had to be put away in the library. Sam Amirtham commented, "Indian art has not yet been brought to the feet of Christ. This we believe is a legitimate field for experimentation. The Indian church needs to get out of its minority complex of fear or limitation."

This was the beginning of a sometimes painful dialectic with the church. Further steps included the use of the Indian bamboo flute (considered by some as Krishna's instrument) and the celebration of such festivals as Pongal (Tamil rather than Christian harvest). Another festival was a Christian dedication in the chapel of such items as pens, books and typewriters, which coincided with the Festival of Saraswati, the goddess of learning, being celebrated in Hindu temples. Similarly, Western candlesticks were replaced by Indian lamps – with a cross put at the top – as in the temples; and dance, also seen as linked with temples, was occasionally used in worship. Sometimes, bread and wine were replaced at the eucharist with chappati and coconut milk, the latter in particular being seen as having Hindu connotations. All these cases made it apparent how difficult it is to change a seminary without changing the church around.

Practical training

From the beginning TTS emphasized practical training. Each student was attached to a fellowship group linked to a local church. Annual two-week exposure programmes took students over their four years into rural society, industrial society, dialogue with other faiths and evangelism. The focus of these fortnights evolved. The rural exposure began with learning about agriculture and progressed to becoming an exposure to the realities of life in the rural context. For most students from rural areas, the industrial course was a first experience of large cities such as Madras. The questions asked of the communities grew more radicalized over the years. Traditional methods of evangelism were increasingly questioned, and eventually the course become exposure to parish life.

The dialogue course involved a journey around temples in Tamilnadu. For the many students who had grown up in mission compounds or entirely Christian villages, this was their first in-depth encounter with Hinduism as a religion. Students were enabled to meet not just an abstract faith but persons who lived by that faith. This was an important challenge to all these minority Christians – and disturbing to some. Hinduism was the religion from which they or their ancestors had converted. Many saw it as an enemy to be feared, an all-pervasive creature seeking to absorb everything around it. In the early days the exposure was to classical Hinduism. Under the influence of the movement for Dalit liberation, many facets of this Hinduism have increasingly been viewed as oppressive, and today the exposure is balanced to include other expressions.

Further interaction with society gradually developed and became part of the requirements for every student training at TTS. The pattern became established that a student would spend his or her first and last years living in the compound, and years two and three outside, in three distinct pro-grammes.

In 1973 five students and one staff member went to live in the slum area just outside the seminary gates. From this began the *Off-Campus Programme* soon required of all students. The aim of this first group was to identify with slum-dwellers and to gain an empathetic understanding of the problems and power structures which oppress them. They hoped to encourage local people to claim their rights and, while not preaching Christ, to live a life-style which was seen as Christian. Such involvement could be costly, and the staff member participating was arrested at one point.

While only a minority went to live in the slums, all students were asked to discern the structural forces affecting human development where they lived outside and to build up relationships with their neighbours. Group living meant engagement with the realities of living in a city and facing questions relating to time, money and personal security. For many students the Off-Campus Programme marked the first time they were living away from a college hostel, or from a mother and a servant who had done everything for them. Some stayed for the first time in the house of a Muslim or Hindu. It was not easy to feed these experiences back into the life of the seminary, but the personal impact could be con-siderable.

In the first half of the third year students went on *Intern-ship* – a four-month programme at first within Tamilnadu but later anywhere within India. Placements were individual and normally not in parishes. The primary aim was to expose the students to the realities of some aspect of Indian society and to induce them to reflect about that experience biblically, the-ologically and sociologically. A variety of situations were chosen: rural and urban, in social work, development, dia-logue, the arts and chaplaincy. As the years went on, an increasing number of interns went to social action groups, some of them Roman Catholic, engaged in "conscientiza-tion" of various groups and often involving radical social analysis.

The months of an internship were often immensely testing for students. Besides writing personal and biblical journals, all were required on their return to make a presentation to fellow students and staff. They raised such questions as: Do we proceed primarily through harmony or confrontation to better the life of the poor? Do church projects really help the very poor? Should pastors be project managers? What are the limitations of pastors in relating to people's movements? Do Western counselling techniques work in the Indian context? Who is actually helped by church educational hostels? Do such places make children more self-reliant? Does the church make women more or less dependent?

The second half of the year was spent on a farm a few miles outside Madurai known as the *Rural Theological Institute* (RTI). This gave students a perspective on the rural context in which many would spend most of their ministry. The initial aim was to run a model farm, with students providing some of the labour, in order to show what could be done for national development. But the infertility of this land largely prevented that, and the farm gradually developed as a second mini-compound, with its own small open-air chapel and seminar rooms in village-style huts. Students became attached to local village churches and engaged in theology in context with one staff member, who lived with them. With the help of such organizations as Bread for the World and World Vision, programmes of health education, creches and small co-operatives were initiated. Soon an extensive programme of non-formal education was begun, adapting the "education for liberation" methods of the Brazilian educator Paulo Freire, including the use of plays and proverbs. In recent years, students have lived in local villages, coming to the farm for corporate learning and reflection each day.

Inevitably, students and staff found themselves involved in issues related to the exploitation of the poor by the rich, the Dalits by caste Hindus. This raised the challenge of whether the church should avoid conflict in order to further its traditional work, including evangelism, or whether the demands of social justice should come first. To the accusations of proselytism raised in some quarters, the response was an acknowledgment that all was done through the enabling power of Jesus Christ but that no invitation to discipleship was offered. A programme called "Congregation-Based Community Development" was introduced to help the church locally to be open to the needs of the wider village through sermon, Bible study and a new lectionary.

As staff and students engaged in critical issues, these experiences became learning occasions for the entire seminary. An example was land ownership. This involved conflict not only with local landlords when land was claimed for landless Dalits, as designated by the government, but also with Madurai temple authorities, who owned land in the vicinity. At one point the seminary's water was turned off for several days under pressure from these landlords, and staff were threatened with arrest. Another example was reflection and planning for a change of marketing strategy by local growers of the sweet-smelling jasmine flower – used everywhere by Tamil women in their hair – who existed at subsistence level while their products made large profits for middle men locally and as far away as Madras. All these involvements were both about the claims of local people and about helping future pastors to reflect on the complexity of issues involved.

In addition to these curricular experiences, TTS initiated a range of projects involving staff and student volunteers. These covered such areas as prison ministry (see the next chapter), work with unemployed young persons, with the elderly, the blind, with servants and in the slums. This meant the seminary compound was never isolated from the world. All could find a home there. Sometimes the seminary became focused on a particular emergency, such as responding to the after-effects of a cyclone in which, as always, it was the poor living in fragile huts who suffered most; or relief work in villages where a dam had burst and many had died. Sociological and theological reflection took place, and the staff member directly involved wrote a moving poem on the subject. Other examples related to caste clashes. Out of

16

these experiences came a growing understanding of the importance of caste, as well as culture and class, as a cause of oppression.

Sam Amirtham quoted C.S. Song's words, "We must see how society challenges the church to re-examine the message of the Bible and restate the nature of the Christian faith." This, he explained, means moving beyond involvement to sharing in the agony, as God's heart aches. Empathy is crucial, not just detached observation. Explanation of the world is not sufficient, transformation is required. The giants of liberation theology were quoted: José Míguez Bonino, "Orthopraxis rather than orthodoxy should be the criterion for theology," and Gustavo Gutiérrez, "All the political theologies, theologies of hope, of revolution and liberation, are not worth one act of genuine solidarity with the exploited social classes."

At times this kind of social engagement shaded into political involvement. In 1977, when Indira Gandhi's Emergency was ended – a time when human rights and freedom of the press had been severely restricted – a Human Rights Club was formed. Its first project was to analyze party manifestos for the coming crucial election. So clear was the issue of freedom at this point that members of the Club – not the whole seminary – issued a statement, distributed outside churches, which offered rather explicit advice on how Christians should vote. Not surprisingly, this raised considerable controversy within churches. Already some had complained, "We do not send our students to you to be taught to look after chickens and cows or to roam around temples. We send them to be trained for the ordained ministry of the church." To this was now added the charge of political interference. Sam Amirtham said that the only answer can be love, for we love the church as our mother. But he used the word "agony" to describe obedience felt to a vision of the kingdom that was coming into conflict with the church.

Work with the churches

From the beginning TTS was concerned to balance professional training for ordained ministry with training for lay leadership. Three specific programmes were initiated, involving both students and staff. *Teaching Mission* took groups to congregations throughout Tamilnadu over weekends. The aim was to teach a revivalist style of music and worship, to introduce new understandings of theology and to learn from the struggles of the congregations. Next followed *TECCA* (Theological Education for Christian Commitment and Action). This did not involve entire congregations but members willing to give time to theological education. Every two years, six centres were chosen. Each was visited six times a year, whether it was half an hour or twelve hours away from Madurai. The first group included 135 persons. The aim was gradually to build up, in the congregations where the students would be pastors, a core of lay people who were in general sympathy with their theological approach. Large numbers have joined this programme over the years, despite the immense commitment it requires from church members and from staff whose weekends are taken up with this task. Later there followed *Rural TECCA*, a parallel programme with less bookish methods.

Through TECCA, students could see the liberating effect of theology on lay people willing to go beyond mere "Bible education" into serious theological reflection. A challenge was raised from this source. "Many people expect the pastor to be a like the Hindu *pujari* (priest), who takes care of the required rituals. For this, a short training would be enough. But is this what the church really needs? Are church members mindless sheep who need officials to pray for them? Or are they the people of God, called to serve God in their daily lives and within the problems facing Indian society? In that case pastors are needed who are able to equip members for their task. For this intensive theological education will be needed."

Local events often brought many Christians and others into the compound. The annual open-air carol service and lantern competition, for which the majority of songs were new ones written each year, drew over a thousand local Christians. Seminars using speakers from a wide range of religious traditions were organized on such themes as the nature and destiny of the human person, the *Tirrukural* (a classic Tamil religious text), grace, justice.

Early in TTS's history a seminar was held with minister- ial committees of each diocese to discuss three questions: What kind of ministers do the churches want? What do they need? What type of ministers do the students want to be? Regular contact with churches was seen as a theological imperative. To enable this, the Friends of Arasaradi was established as a way of building up local moral, prayer and financial support. Students were sent out to visit these ordi- nary members of the church, to listen to them and to interpret the seminary to them.

The relationship of TTS to the church can be described as one of love-hate. It is unambiguously part of the church. The many bishops on its governing council mean that the rela- tionship can never be one of indifference. In 1972, the 25th anniversary of the CSI, young people staged a controversial mock trial of the church. It was bound over for 25 years for failure to love the world, to care for youth, to indigenize, to develop efficient administration, to look after rural churches and to develop special ministries. Much of this critique still holds a quarter century later. But Sam Amirtham shrewdly saw that the fundamental problems are not about the rela- tionship of seminary and church, but about attitudes to involvement in the world, which depends on the understand- ing of salvation.

In this sphere comes the work of the *Mission Institute*. This TTS programme worked in village churches. Participat- ing students combined enabling of village congregations, encouragement of evangelism and involvement in such activities as low-scale medical work. About 35 villages were regularly visited. There was practical reflection on the rela- tionship of dialogue to evangelism, of verbal proclamation of Christ to incarnating the values of the kingdom, of organized evangelism to reaching out in love. The existence of the Institute raised debate throughout the seminary and the church alike about whether the aim should be evangelism or social justice and whether evangelism and social justice can be combined without damage to the one or the other.

The seminary community

From the beginning "a certain freedom in style of life and theology" was encouraged as essential for training mature pastors. This was described as freedom, participation, frankness and independence. Applied to relationships between staff and students, this was contrary to the hierarchical assumptions most of them brought. The principal liked to be called *Annan*, "elder brother," rather than *Ayar*, "Sir" – and this atmosphere spread through the community. Underlying this was the philosophy that all, students and staff, are fellow-learners. To this end, students were represented from an early date on all governing bodies and encouraged to form a student union, which was concerned not just with student rights but also with the welfare of the community. Students took responsibility month by month for organizing the student hostel and cooking. This was no small task, but it helped them to develop leadership skills and financial and administrative acumen.

Sam Amirtham has given examples of how he was challenged to joyful tears by students. A student brought a local slum-dweller into a chapel service one day to speak about his life. The roof of his home had collapsed, and the money to replace it was raised immediately. On another occasion, Amirtham brought a visitor to the chapel at 10:30 pm and switched on the light, only to find four students quietly praying in the dark. He visited a local church incognito and found a student preaching from the Bible and the newspaper and ending with the challenge in the face of grim news, "If you believe in Christ, what would you choose, faith or frustration?" Another student, off campus, used to eat in a local restaurant and noticed that street children and cattle were fighting for the food thrown out in dustbins. He came with the challenge, what should a Christian community do about this?

Sam Amirtham saw that meaningful human community is a pre-condition for living theology and a test for authentic theology. It should be a community that meets for prayer – and there was much of that, formal and informal, from yogic style which was deliberately taught to the freest of prayer. Spirituality is to lead to action and to flow from action – what has sometimes been described ecumenically as "combat spirituality". It should be an open community – and those who came to speak to the TTS community included both the famous and many who would normally be excluded from such a place: prisoners on their way for leave, their spouses on the way to visit, children from the slums who used the light of the classrooms to study in the evenings.

Community also means sharing resources. Since 1977 there has been a symbol of this every Sunday evening, with a common meal in the mango grove for the whole community, each paying 3 percent of their income, regardless of the size of that income or the number of people who eat in their family. This was extended in recent years to include a simpler meal such as villagers would eat as a further sign of a common sharing.

The principle of shared leadership was enunciated from the earliest days. This did not always work, but with the growing range of activities, if leadership was not shared the problems were even greater. The theory remained, as did the concept that a principal should serve for no more than nine years and then revert to the staff. When Sam Amirtham resigned after nine years, he reflected that his ideal of teachers and students as co-learners had been very difficult to realize throughout the institution and that inequalities in social background remained a hindrance. But he set up staff-student groups on personal, ministerial and theological formation to try to learn together.

Staff fellowship and theological support was very strong in the early years. As the size of the seminary and its projects grew, this became more difficult. One TTS staff member wisely reflected that if theological education is to serve church and society, it cannot be treated as a matter of private enterprise and consumption (as in the increasingly prevalent ideology of liberal capitalism). There is a continuing need to share, to interact, to offer mutual critique and inspiration if hope is to grow and enable others to grow.

Reflection on theological education

The theological education strategy at TTS was closely linked with that of the WCC. At the inauguration of the seminary, Eric Nielsen said, "May you have peace of heart and not peace of mind." This combination is not easy, commented Sam Amirtham, but "trusting in the Prince of Peace we move forward". It is this sense of movement that can be felt from the earliest days. The mandate of the WCC's Theological Education Fund (TEF) had said that the gospel should be expressed and ministry undertaken in response to three things: the widespread crisis of faith and search for meaning in life, urgent issues of human development and social justice, and the dialectic between universal technological civilization and local cultural and religious situations.

TTS responded with faculty seminars to mould the curriculum around these three aims. The stated aim was "to understand academic excellence not in the traditional sense of scoring marks in examinations, or faithfully understanding and accepting all that the teacher says, but in a more dynamic sense of being able to relate theological education to the problems of society and the church, and to adapt oneself and be flexible to respond creatively to the challenge of new situations, and grow to be fully formed persons." Sam Amirtham spoke of "Oho!" theology – truth expressed in action, that I *must* do this – replacing "statement-oriented theology". Going beyond that was what Paul Koffler called "Aha!" theology – theology that is living and dynamic and causes surprise.

The action sought is oriented to corporate, religious, cultural and political liberation, as in the Old Testament, which was central to much of the theology at the TTS in the early days – perhaps not surprisingly since its first two principals had both completed doctorates in Old Testament in Germany.

The word "contextualization" entered the WCC's vocabulary after the TEF meeting of 1972. It largely replaced the word "indigenization", which related primarily to cultural traditions, often of the past, while contextualization is about "the capacity to respond meaningfully to the gospel within the framework of one's present situation". TEF suggested that in theological education it should apply to the mission of the church, to educational method and theological approach and to structures.

Further challenges and developments

Around 1975 there was a clear move towards a more radical approach to the questions of society. What had been a concern primarily in terms of compassion at the cultural and social level now became more oriented to structural issues. The call by Asian ecumenical pioneer D.T. Niles to venture into uncharted territory, whether of thought, action or organization, was often cited; and the uncharted territory was seen as that of liberation from all forms of oppression, including oppression fostered by social structures. It was necessary to become disturbers of the theological peace, to bring the church back to a truly biblical theology. The method was to be action-reflection, something now commonplace, but then new and radical and deeply challenging to the churches, as is anything that threatens to disturb the status quo of concentrating on "spiritual works".

Structural developments in this direction followed. A Department of Social Analysis, established to provide training in this area for all theological students, offered a master's degree which was unique in India at the time. Seminars brought together staff and students weekly to integrate theology and praxis around different topics of importance for seminary, church and society. A Department of Communications was established to take up issues of the media and the gospel. Increasing emphasis was placed on questions related to the Dalit community, which makes up about one-fifth of the Indian population but is a clear majority within the church. Dalit issues relating to society, the church and the seminary itself were raised repeatedly; and in the 1990s these became a dominant agenda – not always in a very comfortable way, but a clear continuation of the TTS tradition of confronting issues head-on in the name of the gospel.

By the early 1980s the social programmes were really beginning to bite. This affected the relationship between TTS and the church more profoundly than the kind of controversy associated with the bronzes referred to earlier. Gnana Robinson, the principal at that time, wrote of a clash between light and darkness as the depths of exploitation and oppression were revealed. He challenged the church to climb down off the fence and make a choice between justice and injustice, liberation and oppression, unity and division, poor and rich. Calling for a new spirituality within the seminary, he issued a challenge for an end to caste, community and denominational differences.

Concluding questions

Gnana Robinson wrote, "The seminary is conscious of its primary task, the training of ministers of the churches in South India." In all the vast growth of the seminary, this is surely the crucial test. How far has it succeeded in imparting its priorities to students leaving to work in the church? These priorities must be measured against the needs of the church and the priorities of the gospel in context. If it is not succeeding in this way, it might be providing any number of social projects and yet failing in its primary objective. Sam Amirtham talked about how visions had widened: to include women in training with men, to involve the whole people of God with ministerial candidates, to add dialogue to evangelism, to bring Indian art and music into worship. Human rights was added to service, contextualization to indigenization, social justice to social service. These trends were sharpened during his successor's time.

Sam Amirtham says of the general vision, "We did not catch the vision, we were caught by the vision." In our study of former TTS students, this is the question we shall ask: were they really caught by the vision, or was it merely an interlude in their lives? Did they simply take part in activities, or did a new vision become part of their being? Another crucial question has to do with the extent to which the vision was a practical one. Can graduates, isolated in the church and without the backing of the seminary except for occasional alumni meetings, realistically be expected to incarnate more than a little of what they learned at TTS? And how far was the basic pastoral training, which we have not highlighted above, adequate to the task of equipping them for day-to-day ministry, especially in villages? Or were they encouraged implicitly to think less of these things as they became excited by wider aspects of mission? If this was the case, all could fall apart, since strengthening of the church is crucial to enabling everything else. This has become all the more important as the growth of political Hinduism has added to all the other pressures on India's small minority community of Christians.

When Sam Amirtham resigned, he offered a final prayer, "Lord, we are not what we ought to be, we are not what we could be, but thank you Lord, we are not what we were." Perhaps this could be said to be a prayer for the seminary in 1982, the year we are concerned with and, indeed, for the seminary in 1999, in the year I write. Perhaps it can be a prayer for all who read this book.

3. Ministry to Prisoners: Learning from Experience

In a tiny, broken-down, windowless hut, in which a grown man could not stand up, in a very poor village about 20 kilometres from Madurai, lived a poor woodcutter with four children. His wife had died, and in his bereavement he had taken to drink and selling illicit alcohol. In due course, someone reported this to the police, and he was sentenced to serve six months in Madurai Central Jail. His ten-year-old daughter was left to care for her brothers and sisters. The prison superintendent asked the Jail Ministry of Tamilnadu Theological Seminary to help. Students found places of refuge for all four children. They also counselled the father, still full of grief and bitterness. Reluctantly at first, then with growing enthusiasm, he began to attend the Sunday worship service which students led in the jail. Two-thirds of the congregation were Hindus.

By the time of his release, this prisoner had come to a full faith in Christ. He forgave his betrayers and did not retaliate when attacked on his return to the village. He desired baptism and students went to teach him. To their surprise, he brought others along also. Shortly before Easter, when he was to be baptized, he was rushed to hospital. He died that night, just after receiving baptism. His last words in the hospital were, "I want this with all my heart." His death was a tragedy, but also a victory, and it was resurrection hymns that his fellow villagers heard sung at his funeral by a TTS choir. I thought of St Paul's words, "God chose what is weak in the world to shame the strong, God chose what is low and despised, even the things that are not, to bring low the things that are."

I begin this chapter about the ministry of which I was convenor for seven years with this story of an individual. This ministry, which has continued throughout the 30 years of the seminary's history, is an example of how students learn. Ministry, it has been said, is essentially about "life meeting life". Here this surprising encounter happened across the seemingly vast divide between two institutions, seminary and jail, which are just a few hundred metres apart. Is this ministry about evangelism? Or social work? Is it to minister to Christian prisoners? Is it to encourage change in the conditions in prisons, or in the wider society which cause prisons to be so full and society to be so unreceptive to the prisoner on release? These are fundamental questions.

Sunday visiting and leading worship in the prison school-room have been the core of the work. Social work is carried out to keep families together: arranging education for the children of life prisoners, visiting spouses who have medical, physical and psychological needs, enabling them to visit the prison and making small grants to enable wives to work a little. Teaching has been provided for prisoners studying for degrees. A celebrative Christmas dinner is held each year for the one to two thousand prisoners. There is an annual gathering for prisoners' children, when their fathers are released to the seminary's care for a weekend. There are projects for released prisoners and victim support at the suggestion of particular students. Work has developed with a Junior Jail, where attempts are made to enable young vagrants to return home.

Women students at TTS are involved with the women's prison and with Arulagam (Home of Grace), a project of rehabilitation for women who have been jailed for prostitution. This work began when two such women asked not to go back to their old life. Normally brothel-keepers would be at the gates of the jail to meet women released after serving their sentence for prostitution. These two women were taken instead to TTS by a woman faculty member, and she kept them in her own house until more came and the principal made a college house available. For a year or two, 20 such young women lived in the seminary, joining in social and sports activities and attending Sunday chapel. When the numbers became too large, a home named Arulagam was built nearby. Where else in the world would this happen in a seminary?

TTS is not primarily a social work institution but a place of training for ministry. A project undertaken by a seminary should be judged not only on what it does for its beneficiaries but also on what it contributes to training. Students in the

TTS prison ministry learn much about pastoral care, organization and initiative, financial affairs and fund-raising, co-operating with secular authorities. They are led to consider what is relevant worship for this context. They are challenged by the problems of the poorest in society, as most prisoners are, and to consider the relationship between evangelism, social work and the changing of society. They are led to see that these prisoners, whatever their crimes (and they are often horrific), are still individuals for whom Christ died. Each has a need to receive and give love. Anyone fortunate enough to visit is surprised by the welcome given by nearly all, a far cry from the sombre picture of an Indian jail in the popular mind.

What, then, are the questions that students are led to consider?

Social questions

Visiting a prison makes one conscious of the overwhelming impact of social factors in the lives of the poor. What is the real meaning of freedom or human rights? I think of A. He and his wife are from a high caste, which made the poverty into which they had fallen even harder to bear. They tried to maintain their three children but every avenue seemed blocked. Too proud to beg, the father saw his children wasting away before his eyes. Psychologically disturbed, the parents fed their children some poison normally used to kill bed bugs and then took it themselves. The children died quickly but the dose was not enough for the parents. When the father rushed to the shop to buy more, the parents were arrested. He took the blame and mother remained free, but what kind of freedom? She remained disturbed and was visited by students. He came to Christian faith in prison. But what of the future, of the poverty which will remain when he comes out?

In the jail the students learn how caste penetrates every aspect of life. Caste solidarity leads to the most terrible crimes, including the burning to death of whole families in village huts. Many of the 400 life prisoners are here because

28

in this deeply caste-ridden area it is seen as one's duty to set-
tle scores with violence rather than lose face. While the
castes seem to live together in reasonable harmony as equals
inside the prison they admit that in the village they would
never mix in the same way. How can even a little change be
brought to something so intractable? How can one show that
things can be better in a Christian community – when the
church often seems only to mirror society?

Arulagam raises questions about the sexual exploitation
of women. Women students learn of the plight of homeless
girls who believe they have no option but being involved in
prostitution. One 15-year-old girl I met when I visited in
1997 had been sold by her parents. She had run away from
the brothel in which she had "served" and informed the
police. For protection she had been sent to Arulagam, where
she was found to be HIV-positive. Others have arrived in
Madurai penniless, after running away from home to avoid
abuse, an imposed arranged marriage or the discovery of a
love affair. Brothel owners pick them up at bus stands by
offering food and saris. The story of each raises deep questions about women in family and society. Issues of prejudice
are highlighted when Arulagam attempts to find employment
or marriage for these young women, who are seen by most
people as polluted. Theological students are thus led to
reflect on the special concern of Jesus for women. Yet helping the individual, while a good thing to do, is of only limited benefit if society does not undergo reformation.

Penal questions

Relationships with prison officers are normally good.
However, the authorities have to work within the limits of
painfully inadequate resources. The single welfare officer
who is responsible for 2000 prisoners and their families can
work for only a fraction of them. Prisoners' work is paid for
only in the small cigarettes called *bidis*. Why not pay them
something to save for their families? How much human
potential is wasted because only a few educational opportunities are available? Students can see the abilities of the pris-

oners when they take on leadership of the Sunday congregation. A slogan in the prison schoolroom says that "prison is not a place of punishment but reform", but for this to be a reality far more resources would be needed.

It is sometimes said that the greatest moment of punishment for a prisoner is leaving prison. I think of someone who entered prison semi-literate and who left with a good bachelor's degree, for which theological students had helped him to study. Yet society did not welcome him. Vague promises of work remained vague promises. Had it all been for nothing? Another man returned to his village and found himself completely rejected. He was forced to move on "with nowhere to lay his head". How easy under such circumstances to wish that one were back inside, without responsibility and with three meals a day. Society finds it very hard to forgive.

It is striking how punishment falls on the family of a prisoner, how much a wife may suffer over a decade or more. One such woman came under such immense pressure to remarry that she had to be admitted for psychiatric help. Students gave her support. In another case three children passed into the care of a relative who treated them as slaves. The oldest child tried to drown her siblings in a river and then kill herself. Rescued by the TTS ministry, the three children went to a Christian home. In a third case a mother was left with five children. Her son ran away, but she enabled one daughter to get married, one to become a teacher, one a secretary and one to go to college – all this with only very meagre resources. Often such mothers nearly starve themselves. These look like examples of "the sins of the father being visited on the children". They certainly challenge us to theological reflection.

Further questions are raised by the death penalty. Should the state exact the ultimate penalty in any civilized society? Is any man or woman beyond redemption? Today remission is normally given, but there is agony for the prisoner in awaiting the decision. In earlier days, when capital punishment was regularly carried out, TTS had a special role in ministry to the condemned. The story of a man named Arul ("grace"), who was baptized joyfully through the prison bars a few days before he was executed and who gave his eyes for transplant, something he could do as a new Christian, showed me and others the real meaning of "being born again in Christ".

Theological questions

What do baptism, eucharist, the church mean in a congregation which is two-thirds Hindu, one-third Christian? Some Hindus come regularly to Christian worship in the prison for years. They acknowledge Jesus as Lord, read the Bible daily in a group and in some cases even preach. They write their own prayers and moving songs. They minister to each other. Are these unbaptized persons any less Christian than the baptized? Their careful listening to a sermon or a Bible passage, which is really good news to them, contrasts strikingly with the lack of attention so often evident in churches outside. They are prepared to make a public confession of faith. I think of two high-caste brothers, converted in prison by the ministry of a low-caste *Dhobi* (washerman), who wished to be baptized together on their release to show that in Christ there is no Jew nor Greek, no high caste nor low caste. What is the meaning of baptism in this context? Even if permission is given, should they be baptized away from their families?

Is the eucharist to be a sacrament of unity or division? We decided to open it to "all who love the Lord" in the prison, baptized or unbaptized. The catalyst for this was a convicted murderer who said he could not *feel* forgiven for what he had done just by hearing the words; he needed to share the same cup with Christians. Here we were taken deep into the field of sacramental theology.

Another question is the meaning of sin and its relationship to the Hindu idea of Karma. Many who visit the prison have the feeling, "There but for the grace of God go I." If I had been born in their circumstances, with their overwhelming problems, would I not also be in jail? Why was I given so much and they so little? The popular Hindu answer is clear: it is because of inherited Karma, and nothing can be done about it. The Christian answer is not so determinate. There is corporate sin and greed that makes some so rich and most so poor. But there is also individual responsibility. The Christian believes it need not be so.

Then there are questions of ethics and morality. Many prisoners have lived by a morality which resembles that of parts of the Old Testament. They are in prison not because they have no morality but precisely because their morality is so strict. One prisoner killed a man whose foot brushed against his wife's leg at a wedding. A 70-year-old was imprisoned for killing a young man who forced himself on his daughter. Others are inside because of how they retaliated when their family or caste "honour" was violated. Here it is easy to understand the power of story of the woman taken in adultery and Jesus' words to those who cried revenge. Love and forgiveness seem to stand sharply over against this harsh edifice of law and revenge.

Questions about the work

The superintendent of the prison once asked me, "Why do you help these individuals in a way that costs so much to yourselves? Why not give them all a feast four times a year? That will give you an equal amount of good karma." I explained that we were not visiting the prison to get benefits, but because of Christ's identity with prisoners (Matt. 25) and because he died for all. Others might put the question differently: why help this group, when there are so many innocent poor outside? Again, the reply would refer both to Jesus' specific call to visit prisoners and to the fact that the families of prisoners must be among the poorest in society. Most rich people have the influence to avoid sentence.

Another criticism is that this is only "ambulance" work, helping the victims but not changing society. But as Christians we must address the needs of the victims while working for change. When Jesus promised new life in the kingdom of God, he did not stop healing individuals now.

Others raise the question of evangelism, noting that prison ministry encounters most people at their weakest point. But evangelism is neither the direct nor indirect purpose of the ministry; and all help given is unconditional. Questions of baptism are normally postponed until release. But voluntarily – in Christian terms, through the power of the Spirit – some do respond. Paul responded to Christ when he realized that he was nothing and could rely only on grace. Many prisoners know only too well that they are nothing. If prisoners respond to being listened to and loved, are we to stop listening to and loving them in case they ask where our love and compassion come from?

Finally, it might be said, you cannot help all prisoners, why help any? Why single these out? But it has been said that the Christian who says he or she cannot help everyone, and so helps no one, has ceased to be a Christian at all. Because Jesus could not heal all the lepers in first-century Palestine, that did not mean he did not heal the ten who asked him.

A final reflection

TTS could carry out a ministry in the prison by hiring a worker or two. But this would mean that a dozen future clergy each year would lose the opportunity to be challenged by the critical questions mentioned above. They would lose the opportunity of engagement in pastoral ministry alongside their academic training. They would miss a clear example of action-reflection in theological training. They would not have the kind of chance for memorable encounters with individuals which would remain with them – as indeed they remained with me as a former staff member – many years later.

4. Six Ministries in Tamilnadu

The six persons whose stories are told in this chapter completed their studies at TTS in 1982. They have thus been in ministry now for 17 years. Having followed the ministries of all 19 students in that class, I can say that these six, with their differing backgrounds and experiences, can serve as a representative sample for exploring our central question: has theological education made a difference to their ministry over nearly two decades?

Manickam

I visited Manickam's village (all the names in this chapter are pseudonyms) to attend his wedding. It was a poor village, with a small and fragile church whose walls collapsed during the wedding as the overflowing guests sat on the baked mud window sills. A photograph taken at the wedding is revealing: Manickam is wearing a suit in the scorching heat, his father is wearing a dhoti and a white shirt, his grandfather only a dhoti with bare chest. Manickam's father was a poor cobbler, his mother a cooli worker. Unlike many weddings of TTS students from a "higher" background, this one did not include a dowry or a gift of jewels. The cobbler caste is considered the lowest community even among Dalits, and to this day Manickam cannot drink tea inside the cafe in his own village. I was struck by how far he had come on his life journey.

Large numbers of this caste in Manickam's area became Christians in the early 20th century. But while they make up a third of the church members in this area, only two had become pastors until TTS made it possible for Manickam and two others to train for ministry. Manickam himself never ceases to be amazed at where he is today. It did not happen because his parents dedicated him to ministry: having no role models before them, they never even thought of this possibility. Nor did he sense a "spiritual" call to ministry. Rather, he responded to what he saw as the integrity of certain clergy. Manickam was selected for ministerial training at a time when a temporary schism had arisen among people of his caste, who felt they could only make progress if they formed their own church. Manickam was uneasy about this, feeling that it only provided Hindus an occasion to mock the church. He was determined at TTS to mingle with all, to enable them to understand that someone like him could become a pastor and that in Christ's ministry there could be no slave nor free. At TTS, Manickam built longstanding friendships with people from all backgrounds. One fellow student described him as a walking miracle.

Apart from general training Manickam had three main energizing involvements. (1) Very committed to prison ministry, he learned to overcome fear and not to label people. The balance he struck between loving service and witness through worship became a model for his later pastoral ministry. (2) His internship involved work with a rural group seeking radical social action. His own poor background meant that he had no problem identifying with these people, nor did he worry if there was a bed at night, or whether or not to eat "gruel". He learned new ways of creating awareness through drama and processions. He was impressed with the project workers' practice of daily meditation and simple intercessions, which included Hindus. (3) In the Rural Theological Institute Manickam learned of mission without verbal proclamation, though he wondered whether this was a practical option for someone who was a pastor rather than a project worker.

Manickam's years in TTS gave him confidence to speak in public and to sit with "important" people rather than cower before them. His earlier hatred of Hindus gave way to respect and friendship. He remained convinced of the centrality of Jesus' life, death and resurrection. For those who share that faith, he would encourage baptism, though he is wary of mass conversion movements since they seem to encourage retention of caste within the church.

Returning to his diocese after his time at TTS, Manickam knew he would have to work hard to be accepted. As a pastor, he would be respected by Hindus; what he hoped to find was respect in the church. With his overwhelming commitment to ministry with the poor, he feared that he would, like many pastors, find himself over-involved with the administration and oversight of schools and projects, which would cut him off from the poor. When he was a child, he recalled, his family rarely saw the pastor. He was also eager to recover an appropriate spirituality, which he had found difficult to discover within the expected attendance at the TTS chapel.

In Manickam's first appointment, he had 17 Dalit congregations to look after. Some had buildings, others worshipped outside. The experience of prison ministry had given him confidence to conduct services informally and to use dialogue in sermons, and fortunately his senior pastor encouraged this. In the villages there were no books, and Manickam led worship freely except for communion services, when he encouraged the congregation, who knew only the Lord's Prayer, to repeat prayers after him. While in seminary, he had done much to help prisoners' children find access to education, and he was able to put this experience to good use in these poor communities.

Manickam's next responsibility was as youth officer for nine pastorates. Since there had been little of this work in the past, he began by listening to the real struggles and hopes of young people and arranging Bible study sessions around what he had heard. His biggest effort was a large conference under the theme "Youth on the Way of the Cross". He mobilized TTS staff and students to join him as resource persons and they ran workshops on music, spirituality, village dancing, drama, social awareness and caste issues. A thousand people attended; Hindus took part in the debate on religion and society; and the programme ended with a procession through the town.

Of the 14 poor villages which made up Manickam's next pastorate, many were suffering from pastoral neglect and consequent relapse to Hinduism. He concentrated on the renewal of the church by regular visiting, at least twice a month for each village. Relapses ceased and the income of the pastorate doubled. In the only village with professional people, where militant Hindus were very strong, he was able to construct a church as a symbol of continuing Christian presence. He introduced new music and led a series of talks on great Indian Christians, developing in the process a special interest in church history. On the social side, he worked for the release of the 20 percent of congregation members who were in bonded labour, a condition not far from slavery. He helped them to get loans for mat-weaving – a project which was a success at the time, though it collapsed after Manickam left.

He was pleased in this pastorate to be able to spend about an hour a day with Hindus, something he had resolved to do when he left TTS. He accepted invitations to Hindu functions, as encouraged in TTS, though out of respect for the feelings of his fellow-Christian he did not go into temples. When a high-caste man asked for baptism, he was concerned to balance his response to him with not risking hard-won Hindu friendship. He postponed the potential clash by sitting with the Hindu regularly to study the gospel of Matthew.

Remaining clear of administration and church politics. Manickam developed a discipline of reading, though he could only spare two hours a week for it. He took up the yoga he had learned at TTS. In general, he felt he had been well prepared for village ministry but under-prepared for counselling and leading services.

Manickam then received assistance from the diocese to return to TTS for two years to study for a master's degree in church history. His dissertation was on the schism in his diocese referred to above. Returning to the pastorate, he spent a year ministering in a parish made up of formerly Anglican churches of non-Dalit background – a great change for him – after which he was elected chairman of a large district, most of whose 26,000 members were tea estate workers, 90 percent of them Dalits. He was surprised at this appointment both because of his relative youth and his own social background. In using the post to try to open opportunities for the poorest, he was helped by the fact that the pastors under him had trained at TTS. He was able to build a major church, with cross-caste contributions in money and labour, set up a tribal mission to create awareness and systematize hospital visiting – initiatives which show his all-round approach to ministry.

After two years, however, a new rule was introduced blocking his continuation in this post because he had not been in ministry long enough. Some encouraged him to challenge the rule in court, but he preferred to move. Offered a congregation in a major town with important schools, he preferred instead to return to the villages for a ministry similar to his previous work. While there he was invited by the Christian Conference of Asia to read a paper on Dalits in historical perspective. Encouraged by this, he was allowed to undertake full-time doctoral studies in the local Tamil university. His subject was the history of Dalits in his diocese since the formation of the CSI in 1947.

The results of his research do not make easy reading. Despite a large population increase, Dalit church membership had dropped slightly over these fifty years. He sees the root of the problem in the collapse of grassroots church workers – evangelists, catechists and women workers – whose number dropped from 213 in 1947 to 30 in 1997, while the number of pastors increased from 41 to 113. Many Dalits had reverted to Hinduism, others had moved to sectarian churches.

Having completed this disturbing research, Manickam would have preferred to go back to the villages, but TTS invited him as a teacher of church history. He has important contemporary experience to offer and, in the end, he accepted. He hopes to be part of a new TTS project in holistic mission to the kind of villages which his research has shown are in process of reverting to Hinduism.

Manickam has not lost his sense of wonder at being a pastor. Because of his enthusiasm, hard work and practicality, he involved himself deeply in TTS. His activities there taught him different approaches to mission, which he links with initiatives he has taken in his various village ministries. His friendly ways have brought him close to Hindus, as earlier to prisoners. This kind of encounter interests him far more than the niceties of high theological dialogue.

Without bitterness about how his community has been seen in church and society, Manickam wins respect for his community by his own commitment. He is an example of how much can be achieved when someone comes to the seminary without many presuppositions and without a "churchy" background. He accepts what has been offered with delight and there is a real consistency between his training and his ministry. He has also been fortunate in the support he has received from senior pastors and his bishop: without them this story might not have been so positive.

Jothi

The eldest son of a catechist who was dedicated to ministry, Jothi was given the name of a famous missionary. He owned this for himself as a student when he recovered from a life-threatening illness. He spent three years as a catechist, but found that this ministry was limited in a pastor-centred church. It was with a church-centred piety that Jothi came to TTS, concerned with what he called "spiritual work". He left after four years, unhappy with the church-world distinction and committed to three ministries he had not heard of before – counselling, dialogue and working for social change. Classes on "Other Religions", "Ideologies" and "Human Heritage" had opened his eyes to new worlds. Jesus' ministry was for all, since all are the creation of God. This is what he wanted to share in evangelism. Testimony still has a place, but he was now wary of any kind of evangelism which suggests compulsion.

Jothi points to a number of key periods of learning for him. During his time at TTS, an off-campus year in a city slum confronted him with poverty such as he had never encountered before, along with the reality of disunity in face of struggle. He saw that, as a pastor, he must care for more than the spiritual. This was emphasized in the Rural Theological Institute, where he encountered a greater degree of casteism than he had ever experienced. Through prison ministry he learned not to rush to condemn others. Various responsibilities in the student community taught him the importance of taking a firm decision and sticking with it, recognizing that in leadership it is not possible to please everyone. His internship, during which he was trained in counselling, gave him a new self-understanding and confidence. He was capable now of making decisions in a way that had never been possible before coming to TTS – when he had lived in a mission compound and his parents had even decided what clothes he should buy.

Jothi hoped that the free worship tradition of his area would enable him to introduce the liturgical methods he had learned in TTS. He now blushed to think of the sermons he had preached as a catechist – which were no more than a string of Bible verses taken literally. He was excited by the way texts can be illuminated by biblical study and then applied to the context. He hoped to stay five years in his first parish and to challenge the prominent "theology of blessing", which saw the poor as victims of God's anger. He hoped also to challenge indifference to caste issues, having seen the divisions it caused even within TTS. In this he expected to meet opposition from senior members of the congregation and senior pastors in his area, who would be inclined to see obedience as the highest virtue for a young pastor. To talk often of the poor would elicit from them the accusation that he was more interested in being a social worker than a pastor.

Jothi had a wish to encounter Hindus, to visit their sick, to attend their functions and so to initiate friendship through dialogue. He would have liked to have begun a local Religious Friends Circle such as the one he had known in TTS. But he was well aware of the potential opposition, especially because of the strength of the extreme Hindu RSS movement in this area.

Jothi's first stationing was as assistant within a congregation of 450 families. He enjoyed preaching and carried out a good deal of house visiting and work with youth. When he introduced issues of church and society, however, clashes with leading laymen resulted, and the senior pastor transferred him. Even before that he had become discouraged with the only practical initiative he was able to take to help the poor. When two poor members of the congregation had their houses burned down, he asked the church committee for 200 rupees. They offered just 20. He battled with them and finally got 50. But all this brought his idealism from TTS down to rock bottom.

He remained in his next parish for four years, still not ordained and thus unable to conduct baptism or eucharist. His three churches were completely divided along caste lines. They united only for the communion service. One of the churches was Dalit, and when it was attacked in a communal affray, high-caste Hindus protected the high-caste churches and left the Dalit church unprotected. Jothi would like to have spent time with Hindus, but he knew the congregation would object. He found the only way to listen to a Hindu *Bhajan* (musical performance) was to go into a shop and spend time buying bananas and discussing the music with the Hindu shopkeeper. To get more contact he used to bathe in a common pond, talking with Hindus as he washed, though other pastors criticized him for this. Rather than buy a daily newspaper he went to the village reading room, where he could meet Hindus. He visited a Hindu home to read a political magazine. When he prayed for people of all faiths in the Sunday service, some parishioners disapproved. When asked, he went to Hindu homes to pray for the sick. All this sort of activity was frowned upon by Christians unless it aimed at conversions – about which Jothi was quite wary.

Parishioners were very traditional, and the pressure of sectarian groups around only encouraged this. Jothi began a Bible club which met once a month, for which he received the help of a student, but any changes he initiated had to be very small and were often not lasting – if they were accepted at all. For instance, it was the practice to sing Christmas carols right through November and December "to ward off diseases". Jothi tried to get this confined to Christmas week, saying that medical knowledge had advanced and that the church should celebrate Advent before Christmas. But he failed.

In social service Jothi was able to raise money for leprosy work and took a special collection for Sri Lankan refugees: There was a small project for industrial training and an "Association for Doing Good" which gave educational loans – all worthy, but far from the radical approaches TTS had taught him.

The backbone of Jothi's ministry was visiting – to about a hundred families a month – and he used these visits for both teaching and counselling. He also opened up the house prayer meetings, which had previously been restricted to communicant members, to all. He started a Saturday musical practice group, which learned twenty-five TTS songs. He introduced the TTS musical order into occasional services and also *kalachebbam*, a special type of teaching by song.

In his next church things were easier. The congregation was more open, largely because of the ministry of a saintly former bishop from the village. Jothi started an English medium school, since he felt that learning English was vital for poorer people if they were to make their way. He was involved in the baptism of between 20 and 25 people in three years, including one high-caste person to whom he gave months of preparation. There was much family opposition, but he was able to provide appropriate support from the congregation.

Jothi then went back to TTS to study for a master's degree in communication in order to add to his skills for practical ministry. He felt that these two years helped him in preaching, counselling, dealing with church committees, dialogue and evangelism.

On his return from TTS he took charge of two churches with a membership of 225 families. These included new Christians whom he found less conservative. He felt they needed more visiting, and enjoyed doing this. He also had regular dialogue with Hindus on such subjects as sin and the practical life. There were also some "anonymous Christians" in the area, including one family in which the parents would have liked to go more deeply into the Christian faith but were blocked by teenage children who were influenced by youth activities of the Hindu group RSS. With two other pastors from TTS, Jothi wanted to revive a dialogue centre which a former bishop had started in the diocese, but the current bishop had no interest in this and nothing happened.

As elsewhere, Jothi found it difficult to make progress with congregational leaders on social questions. It took a year to encourage them to initiate a "poor fund"; until then they insisted that there were no local poor. He used sermons and Bible studies to move them forward and encouraged them to dedicate money in thanksgiving for special events. Nevertheless, the rich members would give 10 rupees for the poor and 500 rupees to finance an evangelical convention whose message was that the mainline churches had no spiritual life.

In general Jothi enjoys this ministry. Its bedrock is the expected monthly visits to members. This and preaching is all that they request. To enable them to go further is a very slow process, and Jothi is fortunate to have the kind of temperament that patiently moves them on little by little.

Jothi changed considerably during training. He went to TTS out of the kind of conservative "spiritual" background which he then found himself returning to as a pastor four years later. He was aware that practical realities would constrain his ministry, but these were sharper than he expected, and were exacerbated during the period of several years when he was expected to minister without the authority of ordination. This system is one which risks extinguishing initiative and enthusiasm in young pastors at an age when they could be contributing a great deal. Conformism is encouraged since ordination depends on having a "good" record – which may mean no more than not disturbing the peace. In later years things grew a little easier for Jothi as he gained more authority and could set some of his priorities, particularly in dialogue and social concern. The way he has firmly maintained these ideals, even in the limited way that this is possible, is admirable. He remained loyal to his vision from training, though what he could do was limited by reality.

Joseph

One of fourteen children, Joseph was dedicated to ministry because of his parents' vow, after having four girls, that if a boy was born, he would be so given. After resisting family pressure and teaching in a school for seven years, he finally agreed to try out the ministry by becoming a village catechist in his home town for a year. It was a new experience for him to discover the love shown by villagers; and while he did not like the way they put him on a pedestal, he did sense through them a calling to become a pastor and entered TTS. He felt a vocation to evangelism, inspired by winning back two villages from Hinduism, and he had also seen the great importance of counselling in the village context.

When he left TTS he felt that the church needed renewal before evangelism. He was concerned by the amount of administrative work which pastors not only have but also seem to seek – which is about power and works to the detriment of pastoral ministry. Laypeople, he believed, could look after schools, hostels and the diocesan office. He had also modified his understanding of counselling, no longer seeing it as the pastor giving answers to the villagers' problems but rather as enabling them to tackle their problems themselves. The important skill is creating awareness, which Joseph learned in TTS. When this happens with people of other faiths we are led into dialogue, something which is hopelessly compromised if linked with evangelism.

Traditional social work, according to the parable of the sheep and the goats in Matthew 25, is good, but it is not enough. India is wealthy, but it is the distribution of that wealth which is wrong. In this context the pastor has a role in enabling people to claim the rights that are due to them, but a pastor may not encourage action to claim these rights and then let people down when times are hard. The people must make the decisions, as it is they who will suffer in the conflict. Joseph learned these lessons in the Rural Theological Institute, where he also became aware of a model of the church as a small community with participatory leadership.

This style of leadership – of which he had some experience as a student when managing the TTS canteen – was what he wished to follow in the pastorate as well.

During his internship in Indonesia, Joseph encountered a level of indigenization of the Christian faith which he had not experienced before. He hoped to follow this practice of listening to the cultural background wherever he was posted.

Before attending TTS Joseph had thought of the church as set over against society: society is evil and people need rescuing from it. By the time he completed his studies, he recognized that the church is part of society and that all are responsible for the structural evils in which India is immersed. The Bible should be our guide as we reflect on society, but he no longer used it in the literalist way he had before coming to TTS. Nor should pastors, as they reflect on the church, forget that they too are part of the church. Some TTS graduates rush to sort out problems, without having the patience to analyze them carefully.

Joseph remains evangelical, but the focus of this is now primarily on new life for the poor. The resurrection is not only about life beyond death but also about life now. The good Hindu could have a place in God's kingdom; how else can we think of all the Indians who lived and died before the arrival of the gospel? Numerical church growth is less important than the quality of the church if it is to withstand a resurgent Hinduism and a confident Islam. A church without caste divisions is vital.

Joseph hoped to return to rural ministry and to build up the spirituality of the congregation with a measure of indigenous worship. His time at RTI had given him some ideas on this. He also hoped to be involved in development work, though as a participant, not a project leader.

His first year gave him a good start. He served as an assistant in a town church. The senior pastor offered him much wise counsel and they discussed each sermon together. The pastor's wife was like a mother to Joseph and his young wife; and they had most meals together. Things were more difficult in his next parish, where he remained for four years. The pastorate was characterized by a good deal of group politics, and much personal abuse was directed at Joseph no matter what he tried, though he had good support from his district chairman.

Joseph's problems in this pastorate were centred on the town church. He was much happier in the 21 surrounding village congregations, where he knew every member. The town had a large Hindu temple and monastery; and Joseph tried to start a Religious Friends Circle, as in TTS, aware that there had been much religious tension here. Things began well, with Muslims, Hindus and Christians attending in good numbers. But the Circle came to an end because of the apathy of Christians. Joseph felt very let down. He continued to meet Hindus by giving talks in schools and going to temples when showing round foreign visitors. He went without cassock and was able to engage in dialogue.

In the villages he enabled a number of cultural programmes, dances and dramas which made strong social comment about casteism and exploitation of the poor. He introduced small skits into the middle of sermons as well as the Tamil musical order of worship and *bhajan* style singing, though not in the main church. He inaugurated weekly communication classes during a three-year period. He encouraged the kind of group discussion and decision-making which was typical of TTS, though he discovered how this could rebound when he was forced under group pressure to reinstate a cemetery watchman who had abused a girl: how, he wondered, can we even begin to work for justice? In the villages he also led evangelistic programmes, which were more traditional than he would have liked because of the wishes of village catechists.

After being appointed diocesan youth work co-ordinator, Joseph organized meetings, rallies and processions on such themes as peace, participation and development, dowry, corruption, the arms race, the Sri Lankan problem and caste issues. In these he was able to include Hindu participation. He also led a group of young people to Europe.

Joseph's next parish was in an area full of lorry drivers passing through from North India. He used cassettes and songs to open up a dialogue with them. He found himself becoming more evangelical, not least after his own son was healed after a serious illness. He was now concerned with life beyond death as well as in the present. He found himself accepting the kind of social project work of which he had previously been suspicious as part and parcel of diocesan life. During his seven years in this parish he often found himself drawn into family disputes – at least thirteen major cases that he can remember. He baptized new converts every three months or so, nearly all of them Dalits who had social or educational expectations. Others reverted back to Hinduism, mainly to secure better job opportunities.

In the villages Joseph began a "Human Society Development Programme" for Dalit youth, both Christian and Hindu. He encouraged them to make simple musical instruments and taught them songs, some of which he himself wrote. Some songs encouraged village cleanliness; others made fun of superstitious practices. He encouraged the youth to engage in Hindu-Christian dialogue about questions of mutual interest, religious and otherwise. The group also built a road to the cemetery and secured improvements in the provision of water for all communities.

Next Joseph was transferred to a town pastorate with three churches and many property problems. A schism broke out in one of the churches, which decided to return to "Anglicanism" because of general disaffection with the diocese. This move was not, of course, recognized by the Anglican Communion, of which the Church of South India is now a part. In this assignment it was difficult for Joseph to do anything beyond keeping the church going. He felt surrounded by "principalities and powers", both local and diocesan. Legal cases abounded, into which he was drawn whether he liked it or not. This situation – discouraging for pastors – was typical of his diocese at the time. Also disabling of mission initiatives were the frequent manifestations of caste divisions under various guises. In general, Joseph believes that pastors from TTS were less accepting of the injustices within the church than those from other seminaries.

He moved next to a town where Brahmin and RSS influence was very strong. Here he was able to engage in informal discussion with Hindus, for example in the mechanics workshop where he went often with his motor-bike. All were educated, and his aim was to avoid tension. This meant avoiding any evangelism, and there were no conversions. Rather, he concentrated on avoiding reversions. In one of the neighbouring villages, where Christians had been meeting in a house, he succeeded in building a church on a valuable plot of land on the main road donated by a staunch Hindu who had a vision of a cross surrounded by angels planted in the land he owned. The Hindu benefactor offered a testimony at the opening and he was blessed by the bishop. Joseph also had friendly relations with Muslims who had tensions with Hindus.

Joseph made several attempts at inculturation. In the villages, when the congregation met for eucharist under trees, he would sometimes use a bun and cola from the local shop. He introduced the use of a drum and harmonium into worship, and called someone from TTS to introduce songs to the congregation. The root of ministry, he believed, is pastoral; and this he must get right first. Work in Dalit awareness became one of his priorities, and he was one of two people from his diocese invited to Delhi for a celebration of Dr Ambedkar, the great Dalit leader.

Reflecting on his own training, Joseph recommends that all in his diocese who are considering ministry go to TTS. He remains very concerned about the debilitating caste politics in the church – not only the Dalit/non-Dalit split, but also deep divisions within Dalit communities – and feels these should have been more specifically addressed in training. At the same time, he says, TTS encouraged him to take risks in his work and inspired him to rural ministry. In general, the training was for an holistic ministry rather than one centred on "spiritual works" and evangelism.

Joseph has observed a good deal of change over the last fifteen years. Village traditions are slowly being eroded and urbanization is growing apace, particularly among the young, leaving aged parents suffering and pregnant girls without support. Television in every village has an enormous effect – for good and ill. The hostel system, with Western scholarship help, alienates the young from village life. "Charismatic" churches – which emphasize money and the "theology of blessing" and speak little of the social dimensions of the gospel – have become widespread. Militant Hinduism is now a powerful factor, both religiously and in reducing employment possibilities for minority Christians. This situation, Joseph feels, will strengthen the church in its struggle for survival. As when he went to TTS, he remains committed to evangelism, but it is an evangelism expressed largely in action.

Samuel

Unlike Manickam, Jothi and Joseph, Samuel was born into a wealthy family which was influential in the affairs of the diocese. He had been dedicated to ministry at the age of three days when in a sickly condition. He accepted this as a youth, seeing it primarily as a calling to preaching and evangelism. In preparation he taught Sunday School classes and read Christian books.

When Samuel came to TTS, however, he began to question much of this upbringing. During his internship this questioning came to a head. His placement was in an industrial city – which was a new experience for him – and he was asked to spend a period of time working in a foundry. He found the assignment overwhelming. He could not believe that people could work in such conditions and gave up after a few days. He recognized that he of course had a choice, while the foundry workers had none. Further transformation came as he looked out of the window of his room one morning and saw two children passing: a girl in a smart uniform walking to school, followed by a girl of the same age wearing a ragged dress and carrying a bag of books. This servant girl returned after some time, only to pass by again at noon, now carrying a lunch pack. She returned a third time in the evening to carry the books home. Had God made these two differently?, Samuel wondered. If not, what has humanity done to them? He had similar thoughts as he watched a woman taking water around all their houses from a well. By the evening all she came home with was a handful of tapioca.

At this time Samuel began to read Marx more than the Bible. If he was to work for the alienated, he reflected, he could not become a pastor: being a pastor and giving your life to the poor do not go together. But he put these reservations on hold and returned to his studies in TTS. There he rediscovered the Bible as a radical book, also reading authors like Miranda, Míguez Bonino and Martin Hengel. He found a God who did listen to the cries of the poor, and he felt prepared to suffer for such a God. He faced conflict with his family and diocese when he announced that he would remain a lay person for the moment and work somewhere else. His mother's silence when he asked her to let him go – just as Hannah in the Old Testament had let her son Samuel go – showed him that he could expect little support from home. He decided to search for work where he could contribute to the building of a new India, working with leftists if necessary. His aims had turned full circle from when he entered TTS.

Samuel's internship was matched by other experiences from which he had consciously learned. He was involved with a programme to repatriate Sri Lankan refugees and prevent them from being exploited as they were resettled. He experienced confrontation with thugs. At the Rural Theological Institute he learned of the depths of violence to which landlords would descend to crush the poor and also how authorities and media distorted the truth. As an outspoken member of the TTS Human Rights Forum he learned that the police often behaved no better than thugs. He participated in work in the junior jail and at Arulagam, where the desperate plight of these destitute persons bit into his soul. Internship had been like a conversion, and these other experiences were a consolidation of that change.

Perhaps surprisingly Samuel was also a part of the Mission Institute. He continued to believe in evangelism, and during his final year he wrote a tract entitled "Jesus, Life of the World". The historical Jesus is unique, revealing a God who suffers for the poor. He rose again bodily and, Samuel writes, "I believe deeply that though I die with a thousand wounds, I will rise and come to the Father with these wounds." Such a Jesus must be communicated; otherwise, the field is left to Marxist groups. Christians should join with others – fair-minded Hindus, Muslims and Marxists – in working for the kingdom of God. Dialogue with Hindus is a question of shared lives and friendship in a common cause. He hoped, on leaving TTS, to spend more time in the next few years with non-Christians than Christians. He had also learned Tamil music, which he planned to introduce to people as a way of helping them to greater understanding of themselves and their situation.

Finding work was difficult, but a TTS staff friend helped to locate a position for him in a different language area, where the land was as barren and desolate as his home area was rich and green. Struggling at first, he was animated by the words of Henry Martyn, "Let me burn out for Christ." He joined a health and social work programme and was given a brief to move it in a more radical direction. Drawing on his experience in RTI, he selected nine animators from the ten villages in which he was working, formed two people's associations and gained land for a hundred Dalit families. Samuel felt the pain of personal opposition from the rich. The first confrontation arose over the distribution of rice during a drought. Samuel was obliged to rely on the protection of fifty villagers when the police did not come to his help. Another major case, involving the right of 160 Dalit villagers to drill two wells, led one landlord to offer a bounty of 15,000 rupees to anyone who would kill Samuel. Although he was not connected with a church at this time – there being none in the area – he read the Bible with villagers and animators, but without using theological jargon or a preacher's tone of voice. He discouraged local Hindus from following an itinerant Christian preacher who was promising houses to those who would agree to be baptized. More and more Samuel found himself distanced not only from the official church but also many of his former TTS colleagues, who, he believed, were only using the slogan "Jesus as Liberator" to cover the fact that they were siding with the powerful.

Soon after marriage he left the villages. His wife insisted that they move away, with Samuel's life under threat, when ten huts had already been burned down and there had been eight murders in the area. So ended five years of struggle which had opened up many opportunities, but had also led to a sense of depression and fear. Samuel had been supported by regular meetings with the director of the TTS Social Analysis Department. Yet he felt he had no alternative but to withdraw, since his wife did not understand the struggle he was involved in. What he had learned from these years was that, in order to engage in such ministry, he had to be outside the church's ministry and to seek help from lay people, not pastors.

For the next four years Samuel worked with a large development agency as a project consultant. He tried to shift its emphasis from heavily funded programmes to small-scale local initiatives, and created a study programme for funding workers which specialized in understanding globalization and international economics.

This was followed by five years with the National Christian Council of India. For a time he served as editor of its *Review*, and in Delhi he took a post as political analyst, working on economic issues, justice questions and the relation of the churches to government. In the course of this he met three successive prime ministers on different issues. He played a significant part in organizing the national campaign to obtain Dalit rights for minority Christians, and in this connection he brought Mother Teresa to Delhi and worked with the Catholic Bishops' Conference of India. He also collaborated with the Catholic bishops on several other issues, among them a campaign to introduce Christian personal law. Again, he found himself threatened, this time by extreme Hindu groups, and received many anonymous telephone calls. He played a leading part in campaigning against land mines. He was even made responsible for the Regional Council of Gujarat, an area of great tension in relationship to conversion issues.

In this national position, where he felt he could influence thousands, Samuel found fulfilment. But it was a compromise compared with his earlier idealism. It cut him off from his local roots, both in the villages and in TTS.

In Samuel we see someone who was quite profoundly influenced by TTS in a way that led him away from the ordained ministry. He took theological education very seriously indeed, both formal and informal. The results were striking: his identification with the poorest of the poor and his daily struggle with the consequences of that identification. If he had become a conventional pastor his life would never have been threatened. He received critical support from within TTS; and in the end it was his marriage that led to his move away from the villages. Still, as he worked with the National Christian Council, he made a commendable effort to maintain at a national level the ideals he had held at a local level. If we address to Samuel the question whether theological education made a difference, he would surely answer, Yes, all the difference in the world.

Selvi

While growing up, Selvi never thought of studying in a seminary. As a woman in her context she had only a vague idea of what such an institution was. But, after leaving school and spending three years helping her mother at home, she followed her father's suggestion that she join TTS as an independent student; and she studied there for five years. This was a culture shock for someone who had been brought up not to talk to men at all and had lived in a home where the only concern was church. When Selvi left TTS, she felt committed to pursue whatever ministry was open to her, though she now longed to be a pastor and hoped to bring together other women who had studied at TTS to keep this hope alive. She did not expect to be successful in her lifetime, knowing that the majority of her fellow TTS students were against women's ordination and defended their position with such arguments as, "Women cannot go out alone at night; how can they attend the required meetings and functions?"

Selvi left TTS wishing to share her strengthened faith through sensitive evangelism and dialogue. The latter came naturally to her because of her village background, which had accustomed her to talking woman-to-woman with Hindus. Talk of religion can arise authentically if we are interested in all aspects of life. Her understanding of society had broadened at TTS, and she greatly valued the annual practical training fortnights. She now understood well the difference between social care, important in itself, and the kind of social action she had joined in at TTS. In the area of social care she had worked voluntarily in the junior jail and in a home for abandoned babies, established in a hospital associated with TTS. She understood for the first time what it was like to be brought up without the love of parents.

Practical experience of leading worship was confined to the TTS chapel, because the local churches to which she was attached gave no place in leadership to a woman. In TTS she not only preached three times, but also led the Tamil music service. Her internship was crucial in enabling her to discover a vocation to work with women and to gain confidence in teaching. TTS enabled her to read the Bible systematically, though she found critical methods difficult.

Overall she felt she had entered TTS as a child (though already in her twenties) and had left as a mature woman, realistic about what she could achieve, if anything, in the church, but determined to do something for women in society.

In the ensuing years, however, she was given no chance in her Lutheran church; she merely sat in the pew. She and her family asked several times for some appropriate lay work but nothing was forthcoming. This may have related to her decision to marry someone from another church. She ended up working in turn in TTS-related projects for domestic workers at Arulagam and in the "People's Movement for Women's Rights". This involved her much in counselling, at which she was skilled, and in adult education aimed at enabling excluded women to speak for themselves.

On reflection Selvi felt that what she owed to TTS was the transformation of herself. She saw little hope for women, at least in her church, to use what TTS offered. Her experience in leading in worship was confined to the leading of family prayers. She talked much with Hindus, as she had hoped, but rarely about matters of faith. Her theology books remained in her father's house, as she coped with life as a wife, mother and social worker. She was very good with women and cared well for her husband and children.

In the next period her life grew more and more difficult. Within a short space of time she lost her second baby and her mother. TTS closed the project in which she was working. Her husband had a very insecure job, and she felt under great economic pressure. She organized an employment programme for poor women, stitching towels, and TTS rented her a room in which to do this. But after a couple of years this programme also closed. She sought work in Christian institutions, but all in vain. She became depressed and, under great pressure, family and economic, she died in tragic circumstances, which shocked the close friends she had still from TTS days.

Selvi was a young woman of beauty and courage. She came alive, as she acknowledged, from being in TTS. The church never gave her a chance. She remained faithful to her vision to help women who lived out their lives in poverty, but at the same time she became gradually crushed and dispirited. The problem was not the theological education Selvi had received, but that the church was not ready to receive a woman like her.

James

James was another young man dedicated to ministry by his mother, who named him after a pastor who had inspired her. As he grew up, the Christian life of his grandfather particularly impressed him. During his student days he fell under the influence of an independent evangelical church and found himself in its Bible college, training to be an evangelist and preacher. After six years, wishing to break with this group, he decided to enroll as an independent student at TTS, though warned against this by colleagues.

At TTS James felt no pressure to become what he did not wish to be and learned a balance between evangelism and working in society. This second area was new to him and he found it as biblical as the first. He learned confidence specifically from three involvements. He worked in the nearby slum and learned that people must be helped to self-growth. From the jail ministry he learned not to be judgmental. From the Mission Institute he found that he could combine his old zeal for evangelism with forms of communication that were authentically Tamil. He retained from his past a belief in the ministry of healing, both physical and mental. He continued to believe in the unique role of Christ in redemption, which he wished to share with Hindus, and in baptism, though he was agnostic about the status of the unbaptized "good Hindu". In any case, he was convinced that if Christians expect Hindus to listen to them, dialogue means listening to *their* experience of their gods and practices.

TTS led James to reflect on caste issues, which was vital for ministry in his home area. Only through education and the Bible can hardened attitudes be broken down. He considers counselling to be the most important skill he learned for work in an area where most people are not poor but are unhappy and reluctant to share their problems. He discovered that confidentiality is central – though often not found in pastors.

As an independent student, James had to wait several years after leaving TTS before being ordained. He purchased a lorry and worked for a time in the transport business, but found he could not continue this, because in seeking to be fair to workers, as he had learned at TTS, he was not able to make a profit. He realized that compassion was not enough in the real world.

His first pastoral post was in a 200-year old church, very set in its ways, and relying on money sent by those who had emigrated. Work was routine: home visits, daily services morning and evening, Bible study meetings, youth and women's fellowships, raising money for a new parsonage, looking after two schools. He took an initiative to help the youth organize a petition drive for a new bus route and for better electrical power lines, so that there could be enough light for students to study at night. The church's worship traditions were set, and nothing could be changed; but James did lead Lenten groups outside the houses of congregation members as a witness to those around. He was also able to undertake some counselling, particularly among young people and fellow clergy.

The resurgence of Hinduism in the area led to a campaign to have Hindu children withdrawn from Christian schools. Local evangelism was difficult, but once a year he initiated a programme. Five Hindus were baptized in his three years there. Later he baptized more, mainly Dalits, in an area where the RSS was not active.

This first church taught James to be realistic about what he could achieve and to be faithful to what he could do. In his next post he found his life dominated by the six schools for which he was responsible as administrator. This work took at least 40 percent of his time, and he had to mediate in many disputes, some related to teachers' grievances and transfer issues, others to caste problems among children, aggravated by parents. There were also congregational conflicts, in which he was caught between various factions and the diocese. Since most catechists here were teachers, school and church were tightly knotted together. Schools he found the bane of his ministry, but to cease to be an administrator in that educated area would have meant being looked down on by the teachers in the church. His diocese had about 7000 teachers in church schools, 90 percent of them Christians, 35 higher secondary schools and at least seven colleges. Employment here and in hospitals and projects was vital for Christians.

James spent further years in one of the oldest Christian parishes in Tamilnadu. There were 1500 families and a very tight daily schedule that absorbed all his time: daily eucharist, daily evensong with choir, weddings, house dedications and foundation-stone layings, birthdays, anniversaries, house-warmings, sick visits, hospital work, funeral visits, confirmation classes, school work. Many elderly emigrés returned here to die. There were festivals and missions lasting up to eight days and conventions twice a month. In Lent there was dawn preaching every day and compline each evening. Once a year there was a mass feeding of people of all religions, carrying on a tradition begun by the missionaries. Christmas was celebrated with almost continual worship for two days, ending with baptisms and fireworks.

Here James was too busy to involve himself in diocesan politics. The church as an institution dominated everything and was beautifully kept with its liturgical colours. Worship used almost exclusively the 1662 Anglican Prayer Book. The congregation had sent many missionaries to other parts of India, organizing a home for the mentally disabled, various medical services and a library. More radical social work could not be carried out. Dalit villages around were where the gospel should be preached; meanwhile, members of the caste congregation, with very few exceptions, married only among each other. Dialogue with Hindus happened for James only when travelling outside the parish.

It was to widen his commitment to the gospel that James decided a few years later to return to TTS for a master's degree in communication, undertaken at his own cost. His aim was to learn to communicate better with the more educated people, who were becoming more numerous. He studied subjects such as mass media, cultural media, videography, development and communication, folklore, social sciences and communication. India is rapidly becoming a centre for the mass media and consumer life; and the question confronting the church is how to relate this to the simplicity of life lived and taught by Jesus. James was greatly challenged by his studies in this area. In general, he has kept the strong commitment of his youth, widened his horizons at TTS and maintained his vision within the very real constraints of the very prescribed ministry of his area.

Concluding reflections

The six students whose stories we have told in this chapter left TTS to work in six different areas. Four were ordained, two were not – one by choice, one because she was a woman. All kept a connection with TTS; three returned to study for master's degrees, one later joined the staff, one worked in a TTS project, the other two received regular support in their ministry from TTS staff. Thus for none of the six did the seminary's influence stop on graduation day. Four were dedicated to ministry as infants, but had to own this for themselves later. All came to TTS with evangelical intentions. This was not destroyed by TTS, but combined with a broadened understanding of the gospel which included works of compassion, commitment to social justice and dialogue with people of other faiths. Most of them have discovered counselling as important, undergirding pastoral and mission work. Learning from internship, prison ministry, RTI, the off-campus programme and other experiences has have combined with academic study, particularly biblical study and lessons from living in community, to enable them to leave the seminary with clear goals in ministry.

What has happened subsequently has depended a great deal on the contexts in which they have ministered. Jothi and James entered very conservative areas, where church life is quite circumscribed – in one case by laypeople who assert firm control on the pastor in an ex-Congregational area, in the other by an all-absorbing liturgical life coming out of the Anglican tradition in which little room is left for initiative. In both cases there is a piety that is in some sense admirable but may easily become claustrophobic. Each of these TTS graduates has found it difficult in such a context to maintain their vision, but both have achieved, in a necessarily limited way, some things which can be traced back to their theological education. Perhaps TTS could put more effort into preparing students for this type of context, so that they can find satisfaction in small encouragements and will not have too much sense of disappointment or failure if they cannot bring great change.

Manickam and Joseph have found themselves in more favourable situations where they have been able to do more that can be shown to flow out of their theological education. They have both found it easier to work more intentionally for the poor in villages. Here there are more chances for liturgical and other initiatives. Yet the pressure is always present for transferring pastors who do well to towns or cities, where the ministry is again much more likely to be circumscribed.

What has limited the ministry of most of these six graduates are the realities of church structures and of the position of Christians in the society around. Not much can be done about the latter; and the social context has certainly become more difficult than it was when they left TTS. The sad reality is that the church is very often not enabling but discouraging to young pastors as they try to remain faithful to visions of mission. Some have tried to challenge those structures. The secret is to find a way to do this without seeing their own ministry destroyed by such political battles.

The two graduates who remained lay people have had very different stories. Samuel has had an enormously varied ministry, fulfilling much of what he felt called to in his TTS experiences. Selvi's story was a very sad one. It is replicated, perhaps less dramatically, in several other women trained at TTS. Training women is part of what TTS has pioneered, but it is training them for a church which is still not often ready to receive them.

5. Has TTS Made a Difference?

Apart from the class described in the preceding chapter, I interviewed another 18 TTS graduates who had been in the ministry for between two and fifteen years. This gave a wider geographical spread and a fairly representative sample.

One fact immediately stood out. These 18 pastors, with a combined total of 134 years of ministry, had served in 60 different parishes – an average of about 2 years and 3 months per placement. This could be a very significant deterrent to effective ministry, particularly given the new directions towards which TTS was inspiring students. To rush is often ineffective and sometimes disastrous. Quiet and sustained education and relationships are a sound base for attempting change. Yet pastors are too seldom given enough time for this.

The reasons given for transfer vary. It may be to fill a gap or as part of a general annual transfer; it may be to meet the employment needs of a spouse – in many parts of the world clergy spouses are less and less willing to be full-time unpaid assistants; it may be for the education of children. The latter two reasons militate against placement in rural parishes. Sometimes transfers are made because of a clash between the pastor and diocesan authorities and may involve movement to what is known popularly among clergy as a "punishment" area. Such difficult assignments – chosen for having difficult congregations, or for being especially remote, or for having few Christians – may in fact lead to surprising fulfilment in ministry. More positively, pastors may be transferred because they have special gifts to offer or need new challenges. Yet, as one pastor said, it took him two years to build up a real rapport with parishioners – and then he was regularly transferred. What could he do?

Let me turn now to some specific areas of ministry and mission.

General parish work

The crucial base for any effective ministry in the Indian context (and perhaps in any context) is regular visiting in the homes, not just as a duty but as a potential source of inspiration. One pastor tells of how he was influenced in this by Sam Amirtham and how he – as someone short of stature and of a poor background – has been continually amazed at being accepted into the homes of the members of a large and wealthy city congregation. Another spoke of the need to do ordinary things – sitting, praying and eating with people and, by listening, helping them to heal their wounds. Through organized visiting, this pastor "rescued" forty Dalit families from slipping away to Hinduism, while challenging the wealthier higher-caste members to accept them. Such visiting is also increasingly seen as necessary in the mainline churches because of the growth of sectarian churches. One pastor mentioned that there were 17 such alternative Christian worship centres in the area of his church.

Out of this comes a counselling ministry that is both a giving and a learning experience. When one pastor saw a woman who was in her place in church on the Sunday after her daughter committed suicide, he was challenged to wonder whether he himself could have such faith. Another spoke of his ministry to a woman who cried, "There is no God", as her husband died of industrial burns. Urban pastors spoke of the increase in problems related to alcoholism, drugs and sex, as well as general frustration of city life and its loneliness.

It is a commonplace that youth ministry is vital not just for the future but for the present of the church. It should not be supposed that all young church people are particularly radical in their ideas. One pastor started a youth group for an educated community. Their programme, by their own decision, was a pious one. The young men voted to go on retreat without any young women – lest they be distracted! Their chief interests were evangelism, more youth participation in church and new music. At their retreat they discussed such church-centred subjects as "What do we expect of our pastor?", "How should Christian youth of different sexes meet together in one group?"

Another pastor was concentrating on participatory Bible study, which can have important results if handled well. He concluded that if pastors are really to understand youth and draw out their potential, group dynamics should be included in ministerial training syllabi. Too many Bible study groups take the form of a pastor talking at a group. Another was challenging young people to involve themselves in practical tasks like cleaning the church and encouraged the women's fellowship to provide meals when a youth event was taking place, thus enabling the congregation to be a place of cooperation rather than separate groups.

There are many other examples of specific initiatives by individual pastors. One, following the TTS example, instituted a monthly fellowship meal followed by a debate or other programme – for example, a discussion on "Do we follow the path of Mary or Martha?" (not surprisingly, perhaps, Martha won!). Another introduced discussion about cultural ceremonies such as "ear boring" and "coming of age" for daughters. He encouraged parents to avoid expensive parties and to spend money on feeding and educating daughters. Similarly, he urged that baptisms and confirmations should not be occasions for displaying one's wealth with elaborate entertainment. He recalls a child who had no Christian name because the parents believed they could not yet afford to have her baptized. He tried to teach them that the party after the baptism service is not primarily what baptism is about. He felt he had succeeded when only two out of thirty-six candidates for confirmation had a lavish home function. He also worried about big meals at cottage prayer meetings (the Indian name for house prayers) and requested that only a cup of tea be served. He himself refused money, lavish gifts or large meals when he went to pray in houses. These were small matters, but each required some courage to implement.

TTS graduates have not lagged behind in the regular work of building and renovating churches. One remarked that he had inherited the problem of illegal occupation of a church compound and that is where much of his energy had to be spent. Another spent time scaling down over-ambitious plans for building and enabled the congregation to own something more practical. Another raised the income of the parish by 250 percent. These are examples of pastors who take the basic stewardship of a parish seriously and are not merely carried away by new ideas.

Worship and preaching

What can be done in changing styles of worship and preaching depends as much on the type of church to which a pastor is assigned as on his own views. There is tradition to be respected and the degree of flexibility within that tradition may make change very difficult. This conservatism particularly characterizes former Anglican churches, of which there are many throughout Tamilnadu. One pastor said that the limit of what he could hope to do was occasionally to introduce the CSI Order for Holy Communion. Every service was still from the 1662 Anglican prayer book, decades after the inauguration of the united church. At his previous and more flexible church he had been able to introduce all kinds of variety in worship, following orders of worship that he had filed away from his time in TTS. At the same time, many of the members of his current congregation attend charismatic-style midweek prayer groups. Suspicious of these at first, he decided to go along. He warmed to the atmosphere and, while respecting the style of singing, widened the approach to biblical discussion.

One pastor wrote special liturgies for New Year's Day, Women's Sunday and Youth Sunday. Another did the same for Independence Day and Pongal (the great four-day Tamil harvest festival in January, normally not celebrated in church, where the European pattern of a harvest festival in October is followed). This latter initiative was all the bolder for having happened in a town church normally very resistant to change. The pastor used the occasion to educate the congregation on some rural issues and distributed sugar cane (normal for a Pongal celebration but unheard of in church). He also celebrated Workers' Sunday and informed the congregation about industrial issues. He developed a practice of drawing and displaying in church posters and cartoons, some informative, some raising questions related to social problems, some even challenging the pastor.

Various attempts have been made to enhance the communicative possibilities of sermons and Bible studies. Some pastors have tried question-and-answer sessions, asking the congregation what they remember from the previous week. These have had varied success and are much easier in the informal village context. Others have also used the sermon to draw from the congregation the radical message of Bible readings.

Use of the Tamil Carnatic (South Indian) order of worship has varied. Some who do not themselves have the musical skill to introduce it bring in friends from TTS to do this. Others find congregations resistant, though they may be more open to innovation at services on days other than Sunday. Most have been able to introduce new songs written in TTS, now much loved throughout Tamilnadu.

In general freedom is much greater in the countryside. One pastor was able to introduce meetings for catechists from the many villages in his pastorate, including a common meal and open-air worship, on every night of a full moon. He arranged each month for one village to hold a picnic and open-air eucharist service, with bread and wine handed round from person to person, prayers for healing and anointing with oil. He also held a flag-hoisting festival in Advent each year, using this occasion to confront caste barriers. He began the programme in a high-caste village, where Dalit Christians ate at a common meal, then all went together in procession to the church in the Dalit village where the flag was raised.

Evangelism and dialogue

Views on evangelism are mixed. Some pastors are very critical of it. One insists that the church must itself be reformed before going out to invite others in. Reflecting on his involvement in social work among tribal peoples, one pastor says he is convinced they would have converted if he had invited them, but he did not, believing God would move them to take the initiative if it was his will. Nothing happened, and they have now drifted away from church, leaving him pondering whether he did the right thing. Other pastors are happy with traditional evangelism and point not only to the number of converts who have come into the church through their ministry but also to evidence of the genuineness of such stories. One explained that there had been no adult converts in the previous decade and 21 during his ministry – which he attributed to weekly village visiting. A group of former TTS students were central to considerable church growth in one backward area. While they followed the diocesan policy which aimed at doubling the number of members, they were concerned to balance this with other objectives in ministry.

A pastor who worked with tribal people and in flood relief asked anyone requesting baptism among those who had been helped to wait a year. Similar requests had been made by some 19th-century missionaries, so as not to entangle considerations of humanitarian help with issues of conversion. This is particularly important in the present political climate, where issues of conversion are carefully watched. A city pastor who baptized a high-caste Hindu family warned them that it was their decision and that they should be prepared to carry the cross if required.

Most pastors have found inter-religious dialogue in any formal sense of the term to be difficult. Informally, however, many have taken positive actions, such as visiting Hindu homes at times of marriage and death and praying aloud or silently. One pastor said he remembers in particular a dialogue with a Hindu who worshipped light. After discussing who that light is, they read scripture together. This dialogue took place in the pastor's house, where the high-caste Hindu was willing to meet with Dalit members of the congregation, something not possible on his own territory. He has also held dialogue meetings with youth in a dry river bed, where they discussed national and social questions before religious matters. After several meetings, he introduced scripture reading and prayer.

In some areas churches have faced direct opposition from extreme Hindu groups. Stones have been thrown at churches,

Sunday worship stopped and evangelistic meetings completely disrupted. One pastor used to visit Hindu homes where they had asked for healing prayers secretly and late at night without his cassock. Another bravely faced much criticism from his own people after appointing a Hindu to a post in a church school.

Pastors have used the occasion of the death of an important politician or a Hindu guru as an opportunity for speaking out against divisions between religions. One arranged a major function for international peace with people of other faiths. Others emphasize less high-profile occasions such as conversations with Hindus on a train or with construction workers helping to build a church.

In dialogue it is clearly mistaken to expect anything dramatic. What I have seen among these pastors is a positive attitude to people of other faiths and a willingness to work with them on common projects for the community. They do not see these people as conversion fodder or as people living in perpetual darkness. Where they engage in evangelism, they are involved with sensitivity and conviction, not in a manipulative or arrogant way.

Social ministry

Social ministry can be divided into three main categories: traditional social work, emergency relief and work for social transformation.

Examples of *social work* include projects related to leprosy rehabilitation, building a road or a water tank, setting up a housing development for the poor. One pastor is involved in a large project for tribal peoples, but this includes awareness-building as well as literacy education and health. He has imaginatively included the encouragement of festival, and has insisted that the church should not go it alone but co-operate with the government. Others have started English medium schools. To the objection that these are elitist, supporters argue that it is the poor who suffer most from inadequate government schools, and that the poor need access to English, which is the way forward in today's world. One such school is on a tea estate. Its construction and operation have given the pastor closer contact with Hindus than ever before. He even joined in moving building materials himself. He also started a small library and typing and tailoring classes for unemployed youth. His only problem has been complaints from some Christians that Hindus are included in these projects.

An example of *emergency relief* was the response of one pastor to a sudden flood. This included monthly village meetings to ensure that their new building would not collapse in the next heavy rains. The pastor refused to do the evangelism the congregation members expected, not wanting to exploit the weakness of the villagers. The only worship was among the animators – and one Hindu member chose to take a prominent part in Bible study. Other examples of such relief include a women's fellowship which collected rice, one handful a day each, to raise money for the poor at Christmas, and the collection of money to give a decent funeral to a poor man who had died unloved in a city parish. A pastor who had been involved in prison ministry in TTS received a prisoner's daughter into his parsonage for four months after open heart surgery, which he persuaded the surgeon to carry out free. He involved the congregation and they went on to care for three other severely ill patients.

Perhaps surprisingly in view of its difficulty, some kind of work for *social justice* has been tackled by about half the pastors concerned. One pastor enabled a group of Christian Dalits to join Hindu Dalits in opening up a well that had been taken over by the high caste. Together they walked to the well one morning and drew water. The high-caste persons called the police, but the Dalits won right of access. Several pastors have been engaged in activities with industrial workers. One gained permission to visit workers during their tea breaks and, through dialogue with trade union groups, was able to play a constructive role during industrial disputes. Another held such discussions in his house, facilitated by a TTS staff member who had taught a class on "Understanding Society" and could now demonstrate that this was not just theory. Another felt great disappointment that a similar group collapsed because Hindus accused him falsely of aiming at conversions and some Christians murmured that he was a communist. These complaints led to his being transferred by the church authorities.

Two final examples from the rural context. Two pastors joined together, supported by their diocese, to support a group of Dalits who were grazing their animals on public land when local landlords tried to evict them. Another worked in awareness-building with a group of tribal youth, organizing classes in his own home. Growing in self-confidence, they started four further groups and gained government help for a number of development projects. The pastor protected them from eviction from church land, which they had farmed for a long time. Sadly, when he left, they were removed and a traditional church project begun there.

Even though the stories from this last category are not ones of unqualified success, they do show former students of TTS reflecting and acting on how, with help, the poor can gain justice in their particular context by their own strength.

Relationship with their own and other churches

Few of the pastors have spoken of specific ecumenical activities. Among those who did, the most extensive involved friendship with a group of Jesuits, leading to the sharing of festivals, preaching and concelebration of the eucharist under certain circumstances. Roman Catholics in this location shared their social awareness work with Protestants, who in turn no longer saw Roman Catholics as "another religion". All clergy here are called "Father" by both groups!

A minority have had difficulties with their own church hierarchy. The reasons varied; one was thought to be too involved in social ministry, another to have stood up for a colleague whom he felt victimized, a third to have been ringleader of a group who claimed to be fighting injustice in the church. Others are clear about the problems in the centre of the church, but prefer to concentrate on their local ministry, where they feel they can achieve something. In general, the persons in this group do not give the impression of being "trouble-makers", as those from TTS are sometimes accused of being, but they are prepared to stand up with confidence when they feel there is injustice. They may not always do this as pragmatically or wisely as they might. But they would strongly hold the view that it is not appropriate to talk of injustice in society and ignore what is happening in the church.

Women and ministry

Here the story is not an encouraging one. The number of women pastors is comparatively small, and the responsibilities they are assigned rarely correspond to the training they have received. An example is a woman with two degrees who was kept as a Diocesan women's worker for many years. Although her diocese had accepted women's ordination in principle, her request for ordination was repeatedly rejected, on the grounds that it was not necessary for "women's work" and that there were enough men available for sacramental ministry. Even after she was ordained many years later, she was not given charge of a parish.

Another woman came from a very conservative background and found herself opened up a little by her training. She gained confidence and became more conscious of herself as a woman in ministry. But she was realistic about what would happen when she went back to her own very traditional church. This realism was more than confirmed. The gap between the level of her training and what she has been able to do has been very great. Even male pastors who were former TTS students were not much help. Probably the issue of collaborative ministry between women and men could have been more directly confronted during training. "Women's issues" are not just issues for women students.

General reflections about training

Many pastors spoke of the courage they had gained from their experience in TTS. One commented that this was rooted in the example of the staff and the principal and in the fellowship of the seminary community, which revealed the love of God, which was more important than all the technical learning gained. Some related this to a general encouragement to students to speak up, others to specific facets of seminary life, such as this or that responsibility they had been encouraged to take, or off-campus living, which taught them to be independent in sometimes difficult circumstances. This also gave them natural contact with people of other faiths. Living on the farm was seen as important, not so much because it led to involvement in conflict situations (which did sometimes happen), but because it enabled them to reflect upon village life. More recent graduates spoke more often of "people-organizing" than did those from earlier years.

The training TTS students received in counselling is not always felt to have been adequate, given the importance of this in parish ministry. But one pastor commented that Western models of counselling can put too much emphasis on the individual.

Criticisms are there also. The image of the seminary as a family is a noble one, but if it is followed uncritically, the result can be false loyalties and possibly an exclusivist feeling. There was criticism of dialogue as too academic and training in preaching as too general and not enough related to specific occasions such as marriages and funerals. One pastor said that training for parish life was inadequate, but that it was bound to be so, since only parish life itself can really provide that training. But there is a lack of post-ordination training and structured reflection on ministry. TTS has tried alumni programmes. But in the diocese, it is a matter of good fortune if there is anything significant in terms of ongoing support.

Some questioned the degree to which the seminary should encourage indigenous worship, since many of the methods used, such as dance and the offering of flowers and fruits, cannot easily be reproduced in most parishes. A minority questioned the genuineness of spirituality in TTS, but that is not an unusual reaction in such enclosed institutions.

There was much discussion about the perception of increased polarization between "evangelicals" and "radicals" over the years. While this is true, the same thing has happened in the church. A similar comment applies in the case of the ever-present question of caste: divisions are strongly felt in the seminary, but this reflects the situation in the church. Is it realistic to expect the seminary not to reveal what is found in the church? It has been hard to maintain the family image under the stresses caused by such divisions. Open caste discrimination – usually against Dalits – has been strongly opposed. But there may be implicit or institutional casteism which alienates. Much of this has come into the open in the period after my research and has led to strong – and sometimes controversial – concentration in TTS on Dalit issues.

Whatever specific criticisms there may be, there is a strong loyalty to the seminary at whatever period a pastor was there. It is clear that students have learned as much from the informal as the formal side of training. One underscored that such extra-curricular activities should be seen not as additional or distracting but as central; indeed, he went so far as to say that the prisoners with whom he spent much time were his professors! They taught him to go anywhere and accept anyone; their homes reflected society. Here he learned the whole of ministry. He even learned something of preaching, when he heard an ex-prisoner hold a congregation spellbound by sharing deep personal experiences. Never again was he afraid to speak personally or to use the experiences of others. Another described how he did little during his internship with former mental patients but watch his supervisor, an ordinary man doing extraordinary things. He saw a patience and a slowness to pass judgments, vital for a pastor if he is really to love people. Providing the space for such learning experiences is surely as important as time in the classroom. This, at its best, is what TTS has provided.

The views of church authorities

Mention of TTS does not ordinarily lead to a neutral response, indicating that its former students have made an impact for good or ill, that theological education *has* made a difference. Whether or not this impact is appreciated depends as much on the theology, tradition and practice of the diocese concerned and the personality of those in authority as it does on the performance of the pastors. It is therefore difficult to generalize on the basis of my meetings with 15 people in positions of diocesan authority. But I will try to summarize around certain themes the spectrum of views aired.

Indigenization. All agree that TTS students speak the contemporary Tamil language well. A minority question whether this makes it difficult for some villagers to understand them, but the majority feel that it helps the church to move forward in relating to modern culture. They also appreciate the contribution TTS has made in music. In areas where liturgical strictness is emphasized, there is strong criticism of indigenous practices such as the celebration of Tamil festivals, the breaking of coconuts, the wearing of South Indian dress in leading services and the encouragement of "Hindu style" art. These, it is claimed, confuse congregations surrounded by a Hinduism which seems like a vast ocean about to overwhelm them. Former students have been unable to instigate change in such areas, where substituting ordinary bread for wafers is simply unacceptable and liturgical vestments are prescribed in detail. Another respondent said that the TTS contribution in this field has been "quite excellent". As said above, it depends what one is looking for and from where one is looking.

Indigenization is not always desirable. There are increasing tendencies to call the church "temple", to focus on large "temple" building programmes and to call the pastor "priest", using a very hierarchical and holy term from the local culture, which is a reversal of the strong emphasis on the priesthood of all believers in the constitution of the CSI. A similar point can be made regarding the way episcopacy has developed. It might be expected that former TTS students would be critical of these movements and educate their congregations to question these tendencies. This has not always been the case; their theological education has not always insulated them from participating in such developments.

Social ministry. Here some are very appreciative. As one bishop put it, social justice is "in the nerves" of his pastors who studied at TTS. Another identified their strength as their readiness to do anything for the underprivileged and their ability to react more quickly to crisis situations than most other pastors. Their training in social awareness helps them greatly, as does the example of teachers being directly involved in social action. Another appreciated the way they thought about issues regarding the role of women in church and society.

Some church leaders were more critical. One mentioned the danger of "project mentality": unless there is a project in the place in which they are stationed, some pastors may see their ministry as somehow deficient. Not all are able to develop the resources already in persons without a "project". To address this issue, TTS started an "alumni" project, to provide small seed money grants for local initiatives. But the amount was too insubstantial for much to be achieved. The real question was whether a pastor could mobilize local or government resources rather than rely on foreign funding. Often the money available locally goes primarily into large evangelical conventions or building projects. Church buildings could serve as dual- or multi-purpose buildings, used for certain kinds of projects; they represent an enormous asset throughout South India. But do pastors have the imagination and persuasive skill to bring congregations to the point of endorsing such multiple usage – which, though commonplace in the West, still seems radical in many contexts in India? It could be argued that TTS projects have relied too much on the overseas money which the name of TTS has been able to generate – and therefore are often not reproducible in most local contexts. Even some of TTS's own projects in recent years were too ambitious and failed. There has also been the danger of projects becoming employment agencies or places of safety within the TTS family which shield students from going outside. It might have been better to have students trained by those already involved in society and the church. This has been the strength of the internships, in which TTS has not organized anything but the placement arrangements.

Some see a danger of preaching only the "social gospel", as though that is everything. A senior pastor commented that TTS looks to the development of the whole human being, but in his view it is the government that is responsible for the body and the church which should see to the needs of the soul.

Relationship with the church. This is the area in which the most criticism arises from those in authority. Some complain that pastors coming from TTS are on the lookout for injustice everywhere and, as change is difficult to bring in society, they focus this search on the church and become a disturbing influence. Constitutional questions become central, but the quest for integrity in administration becomes confused with personal grievance. Small pebbles are identified as large rocks. One church leader said former TTS students raise more questions and raise them more quickly than students who have gone to other seminaries. The administration then has a tendency to draw into itself like a tortoise. Disputes of this kind are readily picked up by the secular press, and Hindu opinion is affected. What is achieved? At least disillusionment among lay people; at worst the splitting of the church, as people leave to join sects, tired of disputes.

Fear of breaking the unity of the church is a consistent theme. One side sees the church as an ark on the sea of the world and insists that a fundamental, if not fundamentalist theology is required, not least in response to Hindu fundamentalism. If the mainline seminaries do not offer this, then the 120 independent Bible colleges of Tamilnadu will provide it. Renewal of the church and a revivalist form of preaching are required, not the "trade union" mentality found in at least some former TTS students. Another view, held by a minority, is that it is good that TTS students, with their open and confident manner, point out what is wrong with the church. To be sure, this search for justice and discipline should be tempered by love. The sinner should not be hounded, and we should learn to forgive.

Caste divisions are a deep concern at every level. Some former TTS students have, as pastors, taken a stand against caste-based diocesan politics. Such a group becomes unpopular because of the critique they bring to bear on the majority within the church. One senior person said he would respect such pastors if they had themselves married across caste lines, but they had not. Two bishops, however, commended the lack of caste consciousness among former TTS students and welcomed the lead given.

Evangelism and dialogue. TTS alumni in one diocese were especially commended in this area, in which there was much church growth. A bishop spoke of the danger of a tug-of-war between evangelism and social ministry and of the natural leaning of most former TTS students towards the latter. Another felt that a concern for evangelism was lacking among TTS students and was the monopoly of those from evangelical colleges. Dialogue was mentioned by only one bishop – and this seems to reflect the lack of real commitment to dialogue from most in the church.

General impressions. TTS is commended by some for producing pastors with creativity and initiative with a friendly and informal style. Some among the more conservative church members, however, see this as a sign of insufficient spirituality. Some judge commitment by action, where TTS pastors fare well; others by appearance, where they seem deficient. Easy judgments are made about life-style, and having a particular hair style or wearing a beard or going to the cinema may elicit questions from some about commitment – even though a growing number who criticize film-going pastors themselves have a television, and therefore films, in their own home. It is important for pastors to help congregations through such changes of life-style, and these should be discussed in training.

Some say TTS alumni are good visitors, others that their heart is not in this. Some believe more emphasis should be given to education, in order to enable a congregation to move forward together. One bishop wisely said that too much cannot be expected of a seminary, and that the dioceses should strengthen their selection processes. Problem pastors were often those who showed problems even before entering seminary. Nor do dioceses give enough guidance in the early years of ministry.

Ecumenically, the TTS experience is judged to be one that enables the various traditions within the CSI to mix well and to create respect between the CSI and the Lutheran churches. If a church wants to emphasize its own tradition, it can do that after training. If the ecumenical movement is to move forward, training across churches is vital, as has been the case in India since 1910, when the United Theological College was founded in Bangalore.

Another key reflection is on the place of the Bible in a person's ministry. In TTS there has been an attempt to integrate biblical studies with other disciplines as, for example, in courses on biblical theology. But students have a tendency to wish to compartmentalize again. In preaching they tend to speak thematically and not allow the text to speak for itself. The present principal, Dhyanchand Carr, has developed a programme to enable working pastors to re-equip themselves to reflect biblically in relationship to their contexts, and there are plans to use this with former students and other pastors.

The crucial question remains perhaps whether seminaries give the church the pastors they want or the pastors they need. Is TTS the kind of seminary church leaders want, or is it what the church needs? What is vital is that, if it is what they want or need, then the church provides enough financial support and each diocese owns its teachers on the seminary staff. The seminary has had wide support from ecumenical agencies; it surely deserves the committed support of its governing council, representing its church constituencies. It had this strongly in its foundation and early days; the present principal is challenging them to re-affirm this in the contemporary context. Only thus does it win the credibility to affirm and criticize the seminary and its alumni.

6. The West Midlands Course

The West Midlands Ministerial Training Course was established in the early 1970s to train experienced lay people for non-stipendiary ordained ministry (NSM). The Church of England was a pioneer in developing these alternatives to full-time paid ministry. Some saw their focus within the parish, others within their work context. The latter group became known as Ministers in Secular Employment (MSEs). More recently, a third category has been added: Ordained Local Ministers, licenced to one parish and, unlike those in NSM, not normally deployable elsewhere. The West Midlands Course has trained ministers for all these categories, as well as for stipendiary ministry. There is also provision for a minority of lay persons to study. The majority of students have been Anglicans; others have come from the Methodist Church and the United Reformed Church.

Students training part time must be over 30 years of age, and in recent years about half have been women. They come from a radius of 50 miles from Birmingham. The teaching programme lasts three years and involves one evening a week, seven weekends a year, some Saturdays and a residential period over Holy Week. Between these times, extensive work is required, both reading and writing for a wide range of assessed work and practical placements in parish and secular work. While training within this framework, students live at home and continue their normal employment, making this a very demanding three years.

During the years I was involved in the Course I was given a mandate by the bishops of the West Midlands to revise the programme as a course of contextual theological education. In doing so, my colleagues and I were attempting, not always consciously, to follow what the 1988 Lambeth Conference of Anglican bishops called for: "a shift to a dynamic missionary emphasis going beyond care and nurture to proclamation and service". We were anticipating the 1996 British Methodist report on "The Making of Ministry", with its challenge for "training to be rooted in an all-pervasive sense of mission... to enable ministers to be agents of change and instruments of the kingdom of God".

Educational aims

The course was developed within four main parameters – *experience*, *context*, *tradition*, and *skills*. In addition, students were encouraged to have an *openness to the Spirit of God*, undergirding all they learn as they move on to the future. What follows describes the Course as it was in the late 1980s and early 1990s when the ministers described in the following chapter studied.

Experience

Every student who comes to the Course already has a theology and a spirituality. This experience should not devalued but reflected and built upon. The question to be asked is whether this experience is developing and widening, or is fossilized and rigid.

A ministerial student needs a personal faith that is not just knowledge about God but involves a real encounter with God. He or she should not only have a knowledge of the Bible but also be willing to allow the Bible to encounter him or her. Faith should be reasoned, but not just intellectual, with feeling, but not just emotion. It should be open to a developing understanding of Christ, of the meaning of the incarnation, cross and resurrection, both for the student and for the wider world. As it searches for the purposes of God in creation and history, it should look for truths beyond the superficial, healthily critical of easy answers, always seeking to relate inherited truth to the present context. It should be a reflective faith that can be articulated clearly and not be so deep as to be incommunicable.

The person should have a growing spirituality which can support a future ministry wherever he or she is led. It should be complementary to, not set over against, the corporate church tradition. This spirituality should be communicable by word and action. Prayer should not be world-rejecting, but should bring before God all that ministry is about.

The students are members of families, and their experiences there provide raw data for theological reflection. Their experience in the world of work and community is a gift to be shared with others. The experiences of the group, whose members will be people with all sorts of stories of suffering, struggle, joy and transcendence, and their own interactions as they grow together as a Christian community are also important. At the same time, there will be specific learning experiences, such as a weekend on marriage, singleness and family, when students reflect on their own experience in these areas, as well as looking at what Bible and tradition have to offer. Similarly, their study of the eucharist, for example, will take account of both their own experience of the eucharist and how they reflect on this, and the way in which the eucharist has been seen in the history of the church and of doctrine.

It is vital that students leave the course with a gospel they have *experienced* for themselves, about which they feel sense of mission, so that they have not only been trained in the different functions of ministry, but have a real "joy in believing".

Context

Theology is essentially contextual. Theology relates to its context and the context has a part in shaping theology. This has been so from the beginning. For example, in relating to the church in Corinth, Paul not only applied the gospel to the particular challenges he faced, but also developed his own theology out of those particular encounters. As Dietrich Bonhoeffer lived through the 1930s and 1940s, he applied his understanding of the Bible to the changing situation in Nazi Germany, but that changing story also affected his understanding of Christ and the gospels.

The secular context of the West Midlands is one of multicultural richness. Its cities include large minorities of people of other faiths than Christianity, and an increasing proportion of the active Christians are of Caribbean origin. On the other hand, large areas remain in which nearly all the people in the church and community are white, and the proportion of church-going Christians in the population is small and shrinking. Economically, the West Midlands has suffered from long-term and rapid industrial decline, producing great disparities between rich and poor. The character of employment has changed, with much less emphasis on traditional heavy industry and more on services, leisure and high technology.

Beyond this are the contexts of the nation and the wider world, with an array of issues related to race, nationhood, Europe, peace and justice, third-world debt, inequitable trade relations, the arms trade and ecology. The communications revolution and the microchip affect all aspects of life and undergird globalization. Such issues as abortion, euthanasia, sexual ethics, health care and AIDS are affected by the development of medical technology.

The Course quite intentionally trains students in social analysis early on, so that these skills can be applied to the varying contexts they meet during the course, for example, on weekends spent in rural, small-town and inner-city areas. But it is also underscored that context is never static, and enabling students to relate to change is a vital aspect of the Course.

Tradition

The Christian tradition is a response to what God has done in creation and redemption. God has not left himself without a witness among all peoples, but Christian tradition is about God's revelation to the Jewish people, experienced in their history and recorded in the Jewish Bible/Christian Old Testament. Above all, it is about God's revelation in the birth, life, death and resurrection of Jesus Christ. Tradition begins with scripture, which is the witness to this revelation. But, besides the Bible, the study of the Christian tradition involves all theological disciplines, as that basic tradition is passed on in the history of the church, in the development of doctrine, in the working out of ethical and pastoral theory and practice, and in the formation of particular forms of worship and liturgy, church buildings and art. Understanding how tradition is formed is important in itself as a means of understanding how theology is created. Again, examples of this can be found in the letters of St Paul: the development of the eucharist in Corinth, or the development of Christology in response to particular challenges.

Tradition has been moulded in particular contexts and in relationship to the particular experiences of people and communities. Often it is the encounter with another religion, philosophy or heresy that helps to clarify tradition. This continues throughout church history. We cannot adequately understand the controversies of the Reformation without looking at Luther's personal story in the light of the secular context and history of his time. Ethical truth and practice are not purely relative to present context and personal experience. An understanding of past tradition will help to form present guidelines. So too with the history of doctrine and of liturgy. Not only must we understand the tradition, but we must also understand that its various elements have been growing since New Testament times, sensing this implies a journey of discovery, not a static learning of facts. It is a study of the very rock from which we are hewn.

The hope of the Course is that students will be genuinely enthusiastic as they come to sense, for example, the distinctive theologies of Matthew, Mark, Luke and John, and as they begin to relate those theologies to the situation today, having seen how they related to their original contexts. The first year of the Course majors on tradition in itself, though not to the exclusion of experience and context. Tradition then becomes more applied in the next two years.

There is also the tradition of the contemporary church, whether denominational or ecumenical, parochial, national or worldwide. Here the Course aims to develop a positively critical approach. This means reflecting on the tradition of mission as well as ministry and considering what is good news for today's complex world. It means balancing concern for the tradition of the church with the call to help the coming of the kingdom. Can teachers prepare students to have the imagination to relate their faith and tradition to this rapidly changing world, not glibly but with understanding? Will students leave the Course with some of the tools to do this, not just immediately but as the context changes, as they move from stage to stage through their ministry?

Skills

The questions of "how to preach" and "how to communicate" are important only if there is something to preach or communicate and an understanding of the lives of those whom one is addressing. Speaking eloquently about the poor is of no use if you have not reflected about the poverty of those in front of you and about how the gospel tradition could be good news to them. This having been said, theological education is a time for acquiring skills and for practising and gaining confidence in using them. To be sure, many already have skills, for example, as teachers or social workers, and these skills need now to be oriented in a new direction, rather than retaught. A person with long experience in counselling, for example, needs to think what difference, if any, it makes to counsel as an ordained Christian minister rather than, say, as a member of the Samaritans.

Acquiring skills should not be seen in isolation from experience, context and tradition. For example, a weekend of study of the media may include an exercise in presenting a three-minute radio slot. This is clearly a skill, but it must relate to the context about which the person is speaking as well as the experience of the speaker and the hearers in relating all this to Christian tradition.

Certain skills will be required no matter what ministry a student is to enter in the future and no matter which church he or she will be working with. Other skills are of course specific to certain ministries. Some, though not all, students may need advanced training in counselling or in journalism or in singing Anglican evensong. But all will need skills of theological reflection, leadership and the enabling of lay people.

Openness to the Spirit of God

A key tension in theological education is whether we are preparing students for today's church or tomorrow's, today's world or tomorrow's. Clearly this is not either/or. They will need the discernment to be like the scribe in Jesus' parable, drawing on what is old and what is new, and like the prophet who has the vision to see what God is revealing today in the world and the church and the ability to interpret these signs. These include ecumenical opportunities and what God is doing through women as well as men. They need to be concerned with those outside the church as much as those within, with the immanent as well as the transcendent.

All students should thus have a sense at the end of the Course that they are at the beginning of a journey. Nothing is finished, all is merely started. They will, it is hoped, feel an excitement about that journey and a general unease about how much is left to do, both in terms of learning and of action.

Learning in practice

As an example of how this model of learning can work in practice, let us look in more detail at a unit on the problem of suffering and evil, which was part of a term theme on "creation".

The second and third years of the Course were organized thematically, covering such subjects as creation, incarnation, salvation, life in the Spirit, church in mission and ministry in God's world. The aim was to identify how faith in God as the source and goal of all things relates to experience of work, love and suffering. Using Genesis 1-11 and Colossians as the biblical base, students compared this scriptural material and the concept of the Spirit in creation with different ways of looking at creation and at God's relation to the world and humanity in other religions and cultures. Different cosmologies and the theology of evolution were considered. Theologies of nature and work were drawn from Genesis, and consideration was given to the ecological crisis and realities in the realm of work and employment today. Examples of poetry, painting and music aided reflection on these themes.

As Buddhism has clearly pointed out, only a few human experiences are universal – most fundamentally that we are all born, we all suffer and we all die. Recognizing this, a module on suffering was designed. All students in a class were asked to share one experience of their personal suffering and one from their observation of the wider world, then to suggest what questions these raised for them. Anything could be offered; the only requirement was the avoidance of generalizations and clarity about the specific. The Buddha found his life changed not by general situations but by meeting an individual sick person, seeing a particular ageing soul and witnessing a specific funeral. Jesus' heart went out to particular people with leprosy and to a particular Samaritan woman. Students were encouraged to bring along a press cutting or a video tape.

The personal examples that were offered showed an amazing degree of trust in the class, including for example long-concealed experiences such as having been sexually abused as a child or having discovered that one was adopted, after being abandoned as a child. Others shared poignant situations related to incurable illness in children, accidental death, witnessing a suicide, ministry to those with painful cancer and so on. At the wider level students spoke of natural disasters, of brutal ethnic strife, of living in a world where some (like most in the class) live well while most struggle to survive from day to day.

Most theological disciplines entered into the discussion that arose from this initial sharing. Questions of theodicy here are not posed theoretically but arise naturally from what has been shared. So also reflection on biblical material, especially from the books of Genesis, Deuteronomy, Psalms, Jeremiah, Ezekiel and Job. Students may prepare a drama based on the book of Job. The New Testament becomes central as they consider the implications of incarnation, cross and resurrection for personal and corporate suffering. They may look at specific passages such as the account in John 9 of the man born blind and Jesus' observations in Luke 13:1-5 about the tower which fell on the Galileans. No easy answers here.

They look at how Christian doctrine has approached questions of theodicy throughout history and in the contemporary world, perhaps by reading a book such as John Hick's *Evil and the God of Love*, written from a Western philosophical perspective, or by reading authors who write out of the deep injustices of the two-thirds world. They consider the arguments of modern atheistic philosophers such as Anthony Flew against the existence of God on the basis of the evil in the world and examine how Marxism might analyze issues of corporate suffering. The ideas of other religions also come in – Islam with its focus on the sovereignty of God, Buddhism with its emphasis on detachment within the reality of suffering, classical Hinduism with its link between suffering and *samsara* (the endless cycle of birth and rebirth) and our living in a world of *maya* (illusion).

Consideration is given to the suffering of the Dalit people of India and of people of colour in many contexts. Does God discriminate at birth? Reflection will be provoked on the nature of sin, on the relevance of the idea of original sin within this debate and on the existence or non-existence of "corporate" sin. Christology in context may also be a subject of reflection, perhaps using artwork in which the cross is portrayed in ways that directly reflect people's experiences, as collected in Hans-Ruedi Weber's *On a Friday Noon* (WCC Publications) and in the resource pack *The Christ We Share* (from the Methodist Church, USPG, CMS). Here students encounter such images as the Dalit Christ and the anguished Christ from South America. Hymns and songs and the kind of language they use about the cross are also studied.

At the pastoral level a whole range of issues needs to be tackled. How are we to offer counselling in face of these poignant situations of suffering? When do we speak? When do we keep silent? How do we pray with people who are facing deep suffering? What is the place of intercession in the face of situations such as Kosovo or Rwanda, about which we seem to be able to do nothing? How do we minister liturgically through funerals? What is the nature of a sacramental ministry to the dying and bereaved?

Then there are questions of social analysis. A great deal of the suffering in the world is caused by social inequity or dislocation. Case studies in social analysis can help students to see deaths from flooding in Bangladesh, for example, not as an "act of God" but as a consequence of the inequity of world resource distribution. What may be highlighted includes the greed of those who cut down forests for profit, the need of those who cut down trees for firewood, the corruption of those who use aid for their own purposes, the poverty of those who die because they live in huts while their wealthy neighbours survive in their fine houses. A similar exercise can be applied to almost any situation. The important point is not to stop at the level of analysis, but to go on to ask what can be done about the situation. This is particularly important regarding situations in the local context, such as racism or homelessness.

Church history enters into the course as students look at how the church has responded to poverty in different contexts in various periods of history. Students can look at ecumenical and denominational texts, such as key documents of the World Council of Churches or recent Roman Catholic social encyclicals. The WCC series on "The Church and the Poor", edited by Julio de Santa Ana, is useful in this connection, as well as more recent resources such as the WCC's "Peace to the City" video.

In order to spend time with people caught up in particular situations of suffering, there can be placements for the entire class or for individuals or pairs of students. Examples might be to visit a hospice, an AIDS rehabilitation centre or an advice centre for the unemployed or for persons with disabilities. It is important not to go to such places as spectators but as participant observers. At one point in the Course students were invited to stay in the home of a person of a culture other than their own. One student who spent time with a black family in an urban tenement had to lend them money so that they could buy provisions for breakfast. Conversations during the four days there gave the student an understanding of the plight of an unemployed urban family that no amount of reading could ever provide. In contrast, another student stayed with a very wealthy Asian doctor. While receiving immense hospitality, he nevertheless sensed the great gulf which seemed to be fixed between the circumstances here and those in the overcrowded backstreets of the Asian areas in the inner city. Yet as the days went by, he learned how even here there had been suffering from racism, against which this now rich family had to fight as they made their way upwards.

Another form of direct exposure was inviting visitors from around the world to describe first-hand the situations of suffering in places like Central Africa or South Asia. When questions of "why" arise, as they inevitably do, economic and social analysis can be applied to consider questions of economic organization, world order, terms of trade, international debt. Campaigns such as that of Jubilee 2000 can come alive as a way of social action against evil and suffering.

Even liturgy can enter in, as the group or pairs of persons are asked to prepare an act of worship in response to a disaster in which a number of children have died in a landslide, or a funeral sermon after someone has apparently committed suicide.

An openness to the Spirit of God may lead the occasional student into new directions in ministry from such a module. This may be to ministry within a particular area of suffering, or it may be to remain in the place where he or she is but to act differently. I remember one student who was especially challenged by the deep reality of racism in Western society. Although she lived in a place where nearly all were white, she knew there was much latent racism. She resolved that she would no longer remain silent when any racist remark or joke was made. She would firmly challenge the assumptions behind the words.

I have described this example at some length to show how this kind of integrated training can work and to emphasize that it incorporates all the classical disciplines of theology. The case studies in the following chapter can be measured against this model of training. Have the students continued these methods of reflection, have these learning outcomes been achieved, have these skills of ministry been practised, has the kind of openness to the future described here been displayed in the story of their ministries?

7. Seven Students from West Midlands

In this chapter I have selected seven of the thirty students I surveyed who attended the West Midlands Ministerial Training Course in 1990. They have thus been in ordained ministry for nearly a decade. These four women and three men, engaged in various types of ministry, are examples of how this particular form of training has or has not equipped them for ministry in the rapidly changing context of contemporary Britain.

Sally

When Sally entered theological training she was a vivacious woman in her mid-30s. Her husband was a teacher, and they had two young children. She came from a village congregation nearly 50 miles from Birmingham. Beneath her bubbling exterior, by her own admission, she lacked confidence; and indeed she found herself very surprised at first to be affirmed by the church as a candidate for the Anglican diaconate. Looking back now, she is amazed by how far she has travelled.

At a time when the evangelical side of churches seems to predominate, Sally was one of a minority of people to come to the Course as a "liberal". She was delighted to find this background affirmed in the first two introductory lectures on Old and New Testament studies. She was launched on what she felt was "a radical road", looking at the Old Testament almost as a new book. The thrill she discovered from "questing theology" continued throughout her three years in the Course. Reflecting on this now, she realizes that her passionate enthusiasm became a stumbling block to some of her fellow students. She wonders whether she handled that excitement well, but it was so strong that she is not certain that she would do that any better now.

While Sally came to the Course with a spirituality she describes as "low church", she was persuaded by a Franciscan brother in her first residential Holy Week to seek a spiritual director. She has stayed with this person for the last 12 years and has been continually challenged and nurtured by her. Also influential has been the world-engaged spirituality of the Iona community, to which she was exposed in a residential course led by the Wild Goose music group.

Sally came to understand how deeply ministry is rooted and grounded in context. This was emphasized by the way the Course met for weekends over the three years in different social and church communities. Her parish placement enabled her to see how theological challenges, which are inevitably spiritual challenges, are – or should be – the essence of ministry. Ministry is about the kingdom of God, about enabling people to see it, touch it, dream towards it. It is about challenging the status quo, pointing to reconciliation and enabling people to stand up for themselves before God, like the woman in the gospel with the crippled back. Ministry is the means of doing mission, of being God's partners working for changes towards the kingdom.

For Sally, a weekend in the small town of Malvern was a case of learning by negative example. The subject was an examination of evangelism. Some members engaged in street preaching, singing and tract distribution, while others, including Sally, observed. She was further convinced by this experience that mission is more than telling. She sees it as engaging with real issues, not for purposes of conversion to Christianity, but for the conversion of people's lives to life in its fullness.

On leaving the Course, Sally expected to serve the church as a deacon and had only a lingering hope that women would be able to become priests at some point in her lifetime. She remained excited at being called to ministry at all and, she now reflects, was somewhat naive about the realities of the Church of England. The ensuing nine years she recalls as quite "rough" but also very fulfilling. She found herself playing quite a leading part in "the gender fight". She says that she learned to "play the game" and that restrictions on women have never been much of a block to her. The struggle also gave her a first-hand experience of voicelessness, which opened her eyes as a rich Western European to the many people in our world who are voiceless for various reasons.

Much of this thinking crystallized for Sally at an ecumenical women's conference in Salvador, Brazil, which she attended at the end of her first year in ministry. Inspired by this, she completed a master's degree in women's studies alongside her full-time work. These two experiences pushed her to seek opportunities to serve on diocesan boards and synods. Continuing to grow in confidence, she was elected to the General Synod of the Church of England, and chosen to be a member of the clergy to train others, which she says "keeps her on her theological toes" as she learns from those she is training. She has served in two urban posts in the nine years since her ordination.

In 1993 she was ordained a priest, something that she, like many Anglican women, had not expected. She feels the struggle to achieve this was about justice, about enabling women to live life in greater fullness. It has in turn led her into work with various women's groups, including a self-help group among women who have suffered from abuse and one related to alcoholism. She has combined this with leading special worship services in the ancient cathedral of her diocese, focusing on issues like these as a means of education.

These nine years have been ones of struggle, and there have been times when she has thought of giving up; but overall, she says, her time in ministry has been very rewarding. She has surprised herself by taking quite a high profile in her diocese, recently becoming chair of its Faith in the City Group, which monitors social and community projects in Urban Priority areas. Overall, she says that her greatest satisfaction comes from having seen lives change because she was lucky enough to be there.

As Sally now considers her training in retrospect, she feels that, for her, it was probably as good it could be. Working and training in tandem made it possible to ground her learning in everyday life, something she would have missed if she had gone to a residential theological college as a full-time student. She also valued greatly the breadth of experience and variety of theological and spiritual backgrounds among her fellow students. This diversity is more likely to be present in a regional Course like West Midlands, which takes all selected candidates living in the area, rather than in a Church of England theological college, which tends to attract students from a particular party background within the church.

Andrew

Andrew had to struggle to affirm the choice of the West Midlands Course for his theological training. He was 29, under the minimum age, but he recognized that his personality would not adapt well to a college institution seemingly remote from life. Highly intelligent, he also had an "angry young man" feel about him. Thus, his diocesan adviser wisely agreed to his request. He came to the Course with considerable experience of community work in the inner city and as a very committed and active member of the Labour Party.

Asked about the influences in his training which developed him theologically, Andrew is quite specific. He came dismissing the Old Testament as an archaic embarrassment, but discovered it as the platform for the coming of Jesus. He discovered how to interpret the New Testament for the contemporary context. His view of St Paul was transformed by the book *Jesus of Nazareth, Yesterday and Today* by the Latin American theologian Juan Luis Segundo, which he read in response to a weekend course on Liberation Theology and linked with a term of suggested readings from the Letter to the Romans. Written exegeses, a required part of the Course, taught him how important it is to consider the cultural context not only of biblical writers but also of modern commentators.

Andrew valued well-planned thematic courses which gave an integrated historical understanding of key doctrines, getting to the heart of issues. They also developed in him a healthy scepticism about any supposed golden age of the church: a presentation he gave on the Councils of Nicaea and Chalcedon reminded him of some of the politics of the Lambeth Conference of 1998. The Course's integrated approach helped him to make connections and to see theological training not so much in terms of delivering a curriculum but as addressing questions of life and of God. He has found this to be a solid foundation for teaching, preaching and responding to pastoral situations.

A good presentation on Pentecostalism and encouragement from some of the more charismatically inclined members of the Course allowed some of Andrew's emotional and spiritual sides to come to the fore. He also took a course on Ignatian spirituality and read the meditative books of the Indian Jesuit Anthony de Mello. He was introduced to the Myers-Briggs Personality Analysis, which he has followed up in the ensuing years by becoming qualified as a trainer.

At the centre of his spirituality lies a love of the Old Testament and the way it uses stories to convey theological truths. Thus in preparing sermons, Andrew thinks as much about how he is to say something as about what he is to say. The non-residential rather than monastic style model of training, he believes, has enabled him to develop a prayer discipline for a busy parish situation.

In terms of understanding of ministry, Andrew feels he learned most from his fellow students, with their variety of churchmanship. Liturgy teaching was grounded in present practice as well as in history. His experiences of Holy Week during the Course, based on imaginative use of the great traditions of the church, has made this period a high point in his parish work now. He sees Holy Week as a drama which makes it possible for him to overcome his natural shyness as he acts out the central events to make them real. Parish placements taught him much from traditions alien to him, thanks to the warmth and humanity of his clergy supervisors. A hospital placement helped him to overcome his fear of hospitals (he now is much involved with the Health Service) and revealed to him a model of ministry as presence rather than action. Good training also happened on weekends spent in different parishes, which he found psychologically unsettling, but invaluable in letting him see other communities, their history, geography and social background, and how they saw themselves.

Andrew's understanding of mission underscores the need to listen to what is really being said before responding and to avoid jargon, which leads to misunderstanding. Mission is the work of God, and he is suspicious of materialistic ways of assessing it. Interfaith dialogue, a feature of the West Midlands Ministerial Training Course, made him firmer in his own beliefs and courteous to others of different faiths or no faith.

A weekend spent in critique of the ideas of liberal capitalism has proved useful for his later civic and industrial work. Weekends on evangelism and on baptism, marriage and funerals taught him to start where people are, not where the church is. These offices have become important to him as a chance to meet non-churchgoers, which he finds an enormous privilege. His theological focus on the kingdom of God was reinforced by a weekend looking at the need to balance the individual, the local community and the wider world in his own ministry. The Course encouraged him to emphasize the poor and outcast. Racism awareness challenged him to look at himself and to develop the courage and resources to challenge racism.

When he left the Course, Andrew saw his priority as "comforting the distressed and distressing the comfortable" as he expressed good news to the poor. During his ministerial service he has worked in two parishes, combining the second with industrial chaplaincy, bringing a rich and varied ministry and developing areas on which he had reflected during his Course. He has found himself enjoying the open baptism and marriage policies of these parishes, which he considers to be a form of evangelism. He has provided public support for a local mosque development – for him a matter of inter-religious justice – and half of the pupils in his church school are Muslims. He has been a member of the Community Health Council, articulating the worries of ordinary people. As a school governor he took part in a major review of local schools. These community roles have in turn opened many other doors to him.

While he had expected to find the Church of England as an institution difficult, he says he has been pleasantly surprised that there is room for an "odd ball" such as himself. Crucial have been his "wonderful" training priest and two very understanding and supportive bishops. He has chaired the local ecumenical council and has found it rewarding to hold together tensions, to enable communication and to develop strategies which put the poor at the forefront. He has been engaged in holistic mission to gypsies in the area, baptizing and marrying many, developing a literacy programme, supporting them to gain land rights and combatting the racism against them. Inheriting one parish at a low ebb, he doubled the congregation in four years, with a special ministry to the alienated and bereaved. Paying off a large debt raised morale and gave a new sense of purpose.

Like many who have been there, Andrew observes that former students of the West Midlands Course are "far more enthusiastic than others" about continued training, which suggests that the Course has induced a desire for life-long learning. He himself sees post-ordination training not as a burden, but as relevant to his ongoing pastoral ministry. Thus he has taken up several opportunities for courses and lectures. At the same time, his ongoing involvements have challenged him to further theological reflection.

His disappointments include the reality that his infectious love of study and theology do not attract more people to the study groups he has initiated. He is sad that many people in industrial mission are dismissive of the church which he believes in. He was also disturbed by the attitude to scripture he saw taken by the 1998 Lambeth Conference and the resulting attitudes to gay people.

Michael

Michael had been a Salvation Army officer for about ten years when he felt a call to move out of this community which had meant much to him at a certain stage in his life and to become part of a less restricted church. He chose to join the Methodist ministry. He and his wife – who had five children – resigned from the Salvation Army and were placed in a Methodist circuit during training, an appointment which they continued with two further renewals for 11 years.

Michael looks back on his training period as a time of joyful, permanent and decisive liberation from unsatisfying and narrow conservative evangelical "shackles". He particularly appreciated such books as *Fundamentalism*, by James Barr, *Jesus, God and Man*, by Wolfhart Pannenberg, and *God as Spirit*, by Geoffrey Lampe. He discovered a Wisdom-Logos Christ, which helped him to move towards an inclusive ground for interfaith dialogue. This in turn helped him to grasp the kind of spirituality he found in Hinduism, which he encountered for the first time during a weekend on the Course. He discovered that there are many paths to God and that he had only walked on one.

He now sees service as being at least as important as evangelism, and he does not find a need to convert those of other religions to Christianity. The difference between the gospel and the cultural trappings which are often confused with it became clear to him through his reading of *Christianity Rediscovered: An Epistle from the Masai*, by Vincent Donovan. He learned that theology should precede doctrine, which is a good servant but can be a tyrannical master. He became less interested in the need to be correct or right, realizing that what ultimately matters is not "piety". At the personal level, he learned how to welcome positive criticism and thus to enable it to be creative.

Through preparing an essay "Towards an Understanding of the Priesthood", Michael deepened his understanding of priesthood as a function of ministry within the whole people of God. He has found ministers' fraternals to be helpful places for encountering sharp theological debate and reflection on theological reading. He has attended Day Schools in theology at the university, led by a radical professor whom he first heard on the Course. He has become an expert in the use of the computer within the church, though he has faced some resistance to this.

As a chaplain in children's and maternity hospitals, Michael found an overlap between pastoral care and mission, particularly with the dying and their relatives. He has maintained a love for preaching, which is not always easy for one who has stayed in the same circuit for 11 years. Less encouraging has been the way that his commitment to ecumenism, nurtured on the Course, has met with repeated obstruction or lip service masquerading for real commitment. He had felt a crushing disappointment when a large building scheme had to be abandoned for lack of planning permission.

His short evaluation of the West Midlands Course is that all ministers should be trained in this way. After his previous work and twelve years in ministry, the Course filled a vacuum and provided a depth that he had been longing for but was not yet aware of.

Sue

Sue is a senior school teacher who decided quite consciously to become a Minister in Secular Employment (MSE) and was selected for training on that basis. She combined her vocation to ordained ministry within teaching and parish ministry in a rural area.

Until she joined the West Midlands Course, Sue now reflects, she is not sure that she really knew how to function theologically. During the Course she began to re-evaluate earlier stages in her life and to discover new possibilities. Highlights were shared worship, ecumenical perspectives, contextual weekends throughout the region, ten days at a seminary in Berlin with which the West Midlands Course was twinned, training in counselling from the marriage guidance agency Relate and a number of inspiring teachers. She developed the confidence to explore new directions in worship and spirituality, which had terrified her at first. She learned the value of having a spiritual director, who helped her not to feel guilty about not following ministerial norms.

Sue began to see the school community as "church" in a different way. This did not mean trying to turn school into church, but discovering "secular sacraments". Here she

related to the "religionless Christianity" of Dietrich Bonhoeffer and "the hidden Christ" of "common grace". The
fruit of the Spirit is something discovered in the workplace,
"where there is hope in the face of insecurity and forgiveness
in the face of rejection, where one's identity is proclaimed in
the face of those forces which tend to the destruction of the
self and where there is mutual dependence and forbearance
and charity" (*Working for the Kingdom*, ed. J. Fuller and P.
Vaughan, London, SPCK, p.114). She finds God in the writ-
ings of such poets as T.S. Eliot and R.S. Thomas. It is still
"the plain facts and natural happenings/ that conceal God and
reveal him to us/ little by little under the mind's tooling"
("Emerging", by R.S. Thomas).

After completing the Course she was fortunate to have an
exceptional priest with whom to explore the theoretical and
practical within the context of a parish. All her parish responsibilities were organized in tandem with her teaching post,
and her colleague understood that her secular employment
was the central focus of her ministry. This enabled her to
enjoy her parish work without pressure. She is affirmed in
this by the organization Chrism (Christians in Secular Ministry), in which a central figure is a former member of the
Course who started an MSE group during his studies. Participation in Chrism, which is both ecumenical and national, Sue
sees as essential mission work. The organization states that
its vision is "to help ourselves and others celebrate the presence of God and the holiness of life in our work, and to see
and tell the Christian story there".

Prioritizing her ministry has given Sue new opportunities,
such as the chance to be an occasional resource person at a
laity centre. Colleagues and villagers encourage her by
expressing their conviction that she is different from many
priests and accessible in alternative ways. They also like her
weddings and funerals.

Her greatest frustrations have been at the diocesan level,
although she feels the situation is improving. For the MSE
there is a world of difference between being tolerated or
allowed and actually being encouraged and recognized struc-

turally. As she thinks back on her training, she feels she could not exist as a priest, and particularly as an MSE, without the foundation it gave her. The training was exhausting but vital for her personal development. The time and the place were just right for her.

Jill

Jill is in her second town parish. She came originally to the Course from a vibrant parish with many activities, and the Course enabled her to root that experience within the life of God. Years later, she recalls a particular weekend course on baptism which made clear for her the connection between baptism and eucharist and a vision of the church community gathered and dispersed as a sacrament of God's kingdom. She saw the task of doing theology as the work of the whole people of God. Through her work on the pastoral cycle, micro-analysis and the tools for Bible study, Jill felt equipped to provide resources for a local community seeking to engage in its own theological reflection. Experiences on the Course enabled her to see the role worship plays in shaping and reflecting a community's theology. Then as now she has wrestled with the tension between individual and community in vocational terms, evangelistic terms and ecclesiastical terms.

Jill began her training hoping to enable lay people to engage more fully in the life of the church. Through action and reflection over the ten years since she joined the Course, she has moved from this to a broader understanding of what it is to help a community to discover what could be the good news. The ordained ministry is a sign of the ministry of the kingdom which all Christians share. The minister is to provide resources to the community through education, training and theological reflection and to challenge any tendency to parochialism – enabling all this in such a way that people do not forget that they are loved and valued even when hard issues have to be faced. The ordained minister is often in a position to build bridges into the wider community.

The community which formed the Course affected Jill's own spirituality. The depth of sharing and the quality of relationships incarnated Christ for her. This was a gift that sustained her through some dark times. She retains the vision and the possibilities she glimpsed at that time, which were rooted in openness and honesty of theological engagement. Another highlight she identifies was the contact she had with the Iona Community through the Course.

Jill came to the Course believing that mission is what the church could do for the community. Here evangelism was central. She came to see mission as the church working in partnership with all whose actions or intentions embody the values of the kingdom – peace, justice, equity and love. No longer did she view mission as a separate component built on to the life of a church, but rather as its main function. Worship is to nourish mission, to celebrate its fruits and to assure people of a fresh start when failure has prevented their expressing the life of God among them. She was led to these conclusions through the Course as a whole and through particular exposures to a Family Advice Centre, Industrial Mission and dialogue with people of other faiths.

In the years since her ordination Jill has sometimes been frustrated by the feeling that she has been speaking a foreign language in trying to communicate with clergy who have different expectations and models of church. She sees structures unhelpful for moving churches from "maintenance" to mission, and being female does not help. While models of authority in the church are hierarchical, many lay people operate with a purely pastoral notion of the church, according to which what counts is individual wants being supplied – and even this is not in a therapeutic way. But things may be beginning to change positively, especially in urban settings where risks have to be taken.

After completing the Course Jill has continued to learn through numerous conferences and reading. Travelling to India as one of the placements during the Course widened her vision greatly and led her to an association with the Anglican missionary society USPG, on whose council she has served. She has found supportive friendships within this fellowship, as well as in Iona, Urban Solidarity and the New

Way of Being Church movement which has come out of USPG. She has sought appropriate ways to apply insights from the base communities in Latin America to the British local context. She has learned much from the Industrial Missioner within her team. She says that funerals have also taught her a great deal. She has conducted literally hundreds of them, finding there the gathered stories of the past which reveal God's life in God's people.

Jill has involved herself intentionally in outreach programmes – with the YMCA in holiday projects for disadvantaged children, in liaison with community agencies, in helping to establish a credit union, in contact with schools and as a school governor. She helped a congregation to turn what was virtually a redundant church into a base for neighbourhood mission. She has been part of an action group working for the economic regeneration of a run-down town in her parish. Though a pacifist, she has been chaplain to a branch of the Parachute Regiment Association; and she has had ministries with Rotary, Inner Wheel and the Soroptomists.

Within the church, Jill feels that she has developed a liturgy which sustains people throughout the week and also enables real lamentation and real celebration. She has established various kinds of study and renewal groups and is moving towards a collaborative leadership team involving lay persons, despite obstacles thrown up by those who expect that clergy alone should be leaders in the church. A negative development has been the failure of a project to use a local public house as a base for youth and community outreach.

Jill is convinced that her reflective and active ministry in church and community is rooted in her training, which was contextual to the West Midlands, where she ministers. The tools she gained have helped her to make sense of the context and of her role. The Course gave her, she says, "the framework and the means to go on growing and learning, and for me that is crucial, especially when I see other colleagues locked into difficulties".

Peter

Peter is a paramedic in the National Health Service, a profession he has continued as a Non-Stipendiary Minister. A key moment in his training came when he joined a strike in the NHS and invited other students in the Course to visit his station in order to reflect with him and his fellow workers on the ethical and theological issues raised by a work stoppage in the most caring of professions. Could a Christian, especially one training for the ministry, join his colleagues in this? If not, what does that say about solidarity with a poorly paid and often exploited group? This exposure to applied ethics was one of a series of visits to work places. Another was to a book manufacturing plant whose managing director was a student in the Course. His firm was being taken over by a company from Japan; and he was going to have to declare many redundancies – creating clear ethical dilemmas for a compassionate manager known to be training for the ministry, whose work force was made up of long-standing and loyal employees. A third case study involved a visit to a student's parish where a black person had been murdered in a shopping centre and there were accusations that the police had been involved. The class was able to consider issues of racism in modern Britain around this case study.

Peter came to the West Midlands Course after 20 years of ministry as a Lay Reader. His theological understanding was deepened. He was particularly affected by the gospel of Mark and the study he did of the *ochlos* (the crowd) as a focal point of Jesus' concern. He has returned to this again and again; and it still excites and influences his ministry. Work on black and white studies brought him to face up to the prejudices he had himself inherited from his upbringing. He was led to carry out further work on class structures, both theoretically and as he met them in placements. He found that the Course gave him access to theologians which stimulated him anew. He gained a confidence to stand by his opinions and grew in his ability to evaluate arguments, his own and others.

Like many other students in the Course, Peter was deeply influenced by the version of Celtic spirituality found in Iona and by the use of the symbolic, the visual and the active in holistic worship. The retreats and residential periods he found important for the space they provided for quiet and prayer. He is clear that he does not see himself as a paramedic who is a priest in his spare time – a concept foreign to theology – but as a priest and servant of God who is self-supporting through a paid occupation which gives as much opportunity to minister for Christ as does parish activity.

Perhaps his greatest disappointment is that he has not been given the opportunity within the parish to progress in his ministry. Rather, he has found it undermined, not least because it involves commuting to a place with which he has little daily connection and which is over-staffed, having three stipendiaries, two readers and himself. The senior priest has used him only in limited areas and only for work in which it is difficult to be creative. He senses a generally negative attitude towards his non-stipendiary ministry and feels that as a resource he is being under-used, thus wasting the investment made in his training. He sees little interest in the needs of the whole community and an indifference towards – even sometimes a despising of – the *ochlos*, distancing the church from the wider world. The emphasis seems to be on stipendiary clergy and maintaining the status quo. He feels that Jesus would be weeping over the Church of England as he wept over Jerusalem.

Since completing the Course, Peter has received little encouragement to continue studying and his disillusion with the church as an institution makes him unmotivated in this direction. The nature of his work means that much of his time is spent with the "lost sheep" of God's kingdom – the physically, emotionally and spiritually broken – and this is where he believes God wants him to continue to be. He wonders whether he should continue be a priest of the church, though he knows he will remain a priest of Christ, whether in the church or by joining the lost sheep in the wilderness. He finds fulfilment in counselling those whose lives have been broken in various ways: drug users, single mothers in social care, those bereaved through death and those isolated by rejections. He believes that his training gave him the confidence to be sure of his calling and to cope with the conflict and opposition he now experiences.

Charmaine

Charmaine came to the Course from a very evangelical background. A mother of two in her thirties, vulnerable and unsure of herself in many ways, she was surprised to find herself following such an open course, which many of her friends would consider "too liberal". She had enrolled in the Course in order to remain with her family, and the culture shock of the early months led her to consider withdrawing to go to an evangelical theological college. But she stuck it out. Though it was not always easy, she thus gained a much wider exposure than she would otherwise have known and, she believes, grew inwardly as a person. She also grew in her experience of other spiritualities, some of which she appreciated, others less so, but overall they left her more open to other ideas.

Charmaine's lay ministry had been rooted in music as a guitarist and singer. Her challenge was to move from this to being a pastoral minister. I recall visiting her home church and thinking that it was more like being in a recording studio than a conventional Anglican sanctuary, with free and charismatic worship, not at all bound to or by the book. During the Course, she learned more how worship reflects theology. A week with the Iona group especially taught her this, as did the experience of being a lead singer when Archbishop Desmond Tutu visited Birmingham. This was part of her journey to understand theologies other than her own, through teaching and through exposure to third-world issues. Another exposure was to feminist theology and inclusive language, both of which she took to without being dominated by them; and she hopes to introduce insights from them in her ministry.

As an evangelical, Charmaine had inherited many beliefs which she had never questioned or thought through for herself. "I thought of myself as biblically based," she says, "but in reality I often rooted my theology in what other evangelicals taught, rather than exploring the text of Scripture for myself. Being forced to stand outside the safety of my tradition has given me to space to try other theologies." This has made her wish that more evangelicals would come out of their "ghettos" and commit themselves to the rest of the church, not least so that the rest of the church could see that not all evangelicals are televangelists with no concern for the poor.

Charmaine discovered that mission is much wider than evangelism. Though the latter remains in her heart, she can now agree that mission includes working within the secular structures of society. Though involved in "evangelical projects", she looks beyond these to the leading and equipping of the church to see themselves as "missionary congregations".

Leaving the Course she was somewhat confused about her understanding of ministry and where she was going. She wrote at the time that "the account of Jesus in the wilderness preparing for public ministry has taken on a new meaning for me, and even the wilderness with Jesus can become a fruitful and beautiful place." She hoped that life in the parish would help her to sort this out, as she offered her gifts to the church. Since then she has been in three parishes and is presently vicar in a country parish. She is still trying to find what she considers a creative role, while fulfilling the duties of a parish incumbent. She finds some resistance to her ideas, but after a difficult start she has grown in confidence, enabling her to continue to learn from a secure base and to enable others. She considers herself better at "doing a beginning work" than at being part of a great successful team. "God's plans are different from my expectations – and better!", she reflects. She wisely concludes that she has found creativity in new ways, and talked to me about a very sad pastoral case that she had handled with confidence and sensitivity.

Overall, Charmaine considers that the integrated teaching approach of the course, on reflection, was not systematic enough in biblical and theological areas and that there was too much learning from the experience of the group. She felt a mixture of great frustration and thrilling new discovery. She would have preferred a more didactic programme and is now working on a part-time bachelor's degree in applied theology to complement her earlier training. On the other hand, she feels that exposure during the Course to a great variety of students equipped her well for the reality of the Church of England and its diversity of ministers.

8. Does It Make a Difference?

Asked recently which of my jobs has been most influential in my own ministry, I replied without hesitation that it had been my time at TTS. Having taught there means that theological education has made a great deal of difference to me as a teacher. This difference affected me quite specifically as I considered the West Midlands Ministerial Training Course, even though the context was very different and, since this was a part-time Course, what could be done was more limited. So, too, in coming to an institution at Queen's College which is concerned with education, not with action in mission, I faced this new challenge with many of the principles of education I learned at TTS in mind: the centrality of mission as well as ministry, the importance of the context of church and society, the reality – both theological and practical – that we live in a multi-religious world, the fact that Western theology is now just one area on the global theological map.

More deeply, I came convinced of the centrality of biblical reflection in theological study, having felt the vigour of the way this was applied in TTS. I will be forever thankful for my British academic training in biblical languages and biblical criticism, but it was in TTS that I became excited about applying the Bible to life. I also became convinced at TTS that worship and spirituality are not in a separate compartment from mission and engagement with the world, but that both flow into each other. I came to recognize that students learn most from their reflection on challenging experiences. At TTS this was mostly reflection on new experiences encountered during the four years; in the West Midlands Ministerial Training Course the subject of reflection was perhaps more often what students brought with them than the new things they experienced. Moreover, developing a fellowship of learning such as I experienced at TTS was central to what we were trying to achieve with the West Midlands Course. Being part of the latter was like being part of a movement: community, relationships and journeying together were all part of learning, providing the necessary protection and motivation when that journey became very tough for the individual within the group, which happened often, since the Course came on top of all the normal pressures of life.

The question of the *difference* made by theological education can be seen as a double question: does it make a difference to those who undertake theological training? and does it make a difference to the church which receives them? Perhaps a prior question has to do with whether it is intended to make a difference. Some may consider that the role of education is to consolidate what people are and to prepare them to maintain a church which is happy to be where it is and has no desire for pastors who will "make a difference" by disturbing the status quo. Students preparing for such a church are often ready to learn their craft in a way that enables them effectively to preserve what is there.

But if we want theological education to make a difference, the question becomes "difference in what way?". Here the answer will depend on the context. For a church under persecution, it may be to enable clergy to remain faithful under extreme stress, to teach their lay people to remain firm and pass on the faith to their children. For the church in the West, it may be to bring life and renewal to declining congregations, so that they regain a sense of mission; to facilitate members to reflect biblically and theologically within the complex world of the rapidly changing secular society; to provide pastoral care to those who feel lost in such a society; to engage sensitively with that secular and multi-cultural society, witnessing to Christ by actions as much as words.

In a society such as India, the aim may be to enable congregations to own their Indian-ness in worship, spirituality and theology; to give confidence to minority Christians in face of the kind of provocations they face in an increasingly divided society; to enable their people to contribute to the development of modern India; to engage constructively where possible with people of other faiths; to enable the poor and excluded to fight for their justified place within society and the church; to help village congregations especially to remain faithful by building up appropriate structures of pastoral care; to engage in sensitive evangelism. It is in relation to such aims that we need to measure whether our examples have made a difference – to the students and to the church. Readers may make their own list of objectives for theological training in their context, to ask if theological education makes a difference where they are.

Sam Amirtham once said that he knew that about 25 percent of his students would leave as they came, unaffected by their education, and 25 percent would imbibe everything new that was given and make it their own. The key question was whether the middle 50 percent could be moved significantly towards change. My research would suggest that he is about right. Those in the first group obtain their qualifications, insulate themselves from any decisive impact from their teachers or fellow students or from the learning experiences offered to them and return to a church which is probably only too relieved to take them back as pastors "untouched by TTS". Their preaching remains more or less as before they came, their Bible reading is pietistic and unshaken by modern scholarship or radical application, their pastoral care is perhaps faithful but unrelated to any corporate sense of what entraps people, their participation in the wider church is conformist and uncritical. In short, their horizons are for the most part limited by the boundaries of the church and largely undisturbed by the world.

Those in the other 25 percent group become leaders within the various spheres of seminary life. From there, they gain the experience that enables them to look creatively at how to ground their learning in their pastoral ministry. They continue their reading and theological reflection around the experiences of ministry and become activists and resource persons within their dioceses. They are likely to go on to further studies at TTS or elsewhere. Some will become seminary teachers or leaders in the church.

The middle 50 percent – the group who could go either way – are those about whom the success of a seminary should be judged. If the learning experience is positive, they move towards the changed 25 percent; if not, they will become similar to the first group and conform to whatever they find in the church.

Besides the personalities of the students concerned and their response to the education they receive, two other factors are key influences. These are the context of the church and the context of society around. We need to distinguish here between the diocese and the church at the local level. A pastor may go to an affirming diocese, where the leadership provides encouragement, but be assigned to a local parish which does not provide a climate conducive to carrying out new ideas. The reaction to any suggested innovation may be to point out every conceivable difficulty, or to acknowledge that this might work elsewhere but not here, or simply to say No. Such innate conservatism may stifle all initiative and take the life out of someone's ministry.

But this is unlikely to happen to a pastor in two consecutive parishes. Moving may open up opportunities, provided that the vision has not been lost and the diocesan climate is hopeful. More difficult is the situation in which the diocese appears as oppressive, where morale is low, and where new directions are seen as threats and innovators are suspected of being trouble-makers. Under such circumstances, it is very easy for a pastor to draw into a shell and opt for the line of least resistance. Another diocesan context which inhibits change is where tradition is so strong and the ways of carrying out ministry so set that there is little space for initiative. In these cases, one should not be too quick to judge that theological education has not made a difference. One should look to what the person does when there is a little scope for doing anything. One should look at how these pastors' reflection is continuing and how far they are remaining outward-looking when issues come at them from beyond the church, not despising the small things that keep hope alive and indicate the direction in which they are travelling.

For others, the church context is easier. More can be expected of a pastor in a parish where he or she has a certain freedom to make decisions and to lead. In India, city contexts are normally more difficult than rural parishes in this respect.

While urban people may be very educated, this does not mean that they find change any easier; indeed, it is often precisely the opposite, as they feel safe in a parish environment which sees to their spiritual needs while they make a success of the rest of their life. It takes a brave and able pastor to challenge the economic power of landlords or business people in the interests of the poor within the congregation, not to mention those from outside who may not even be Christians. Experience and teaching in TTS may have been effective in indicating what should be done; much more difficult is to do it.

As for the context of society, this has changed rapidly in India over the years since 1982. What is important is that theological education prepares future pastors to read the signs of the times and gives them the tools of social analysis, of understanding society and of biblical reflection. These can then be applied to changing realities as guides to appropriate action. The Indian middle class has grown considerably in the past 15 years and now has access to facilities unheard of twenty years ago, thanks to the liberalization of the economy and the communications revolution. At the same time, the poor have grown relatively poorer. Caste and religion, far from withering away, have grown stronger because of the weakening of all Indian political parties and the need for local vote banks. *Hindutva*, once the cry of an eccentric minority on the right, has become a dominant slogan in an India approaching the millennium, an India more likely to boast of its nuclear weapons than of the Gandhian philosophy of nonviolence.

It is in the context of such changes and more that ministry now takes place. It is certainly no easier for pastors and congregations to survive, let alone to grow. Making a real difference in people's lives has become more difficult. For theological education to make a difference it must prepare students for a flexible response to such changes. My impression is that TTS has largely achieved this, not least because of the work of the Social Analysis Department and the way such programmes as internship and the Rural Theological Institute encourage reflection about contemporary realities, teaching skills that are transferable to ever-developing situations. Perhaps the key prayer they need to know is that of Reinhold Niebuhr, "Lord, grant us the courage to change the things we can change, the serenity to accept the things we cannot change, and the wisdom to know the difference."

Turning to Britain, we see a rather different church context. Here it makes far less difference in which diocese a pastor is ministering; church tradition depends more on the parish. The central structures of the church and the power of the authorities are not so inhibiting as in the CSI. It is easier, in other words, to bring change if the parish context is open and there are cooperative lay persons. But the parameters of ministry and the vision of pastors are not normally as wide. The focus tends to be on pastoral ministry rather than mission outside. This is partly because of how theological education is done, partly because of the way the church is.

When I surveyed my students in TTS about their expectations on leaving seminary, the greatest numbers by far saw their priorities in some area of mission, whether evangelism, social work, social justice or interfaith dialogue. When I put the same questions to students from the West Midlands Ministerial Training Course and Queen's College, I found that preaching, administering the sacraments or pastoral counselling were at the forefront of the expectations of almost all (which one they chose depends on whether they are Methodists, Anglicans or women respectively). Few chose the "mission" options on my list. Some hardly seemed to understand them. The Indian students understood the pastoral options well and certainly considered them important. But their highest priority lay elsewhere.

Perhaps we see here where theological education most makes a difference in each case. Some would consider that TTS's concentration on wider social issues detracts from pastoral education. The result may be that pastors in the parish feel they have failed if they have not been effective in the mission areas of their work, even if they succeed in pastoral ministry. In England, those who are effective pastors in the parish gain a high sense of job satisfaction even if they do little mission. Moreover, in Western Europe the state has taken responsibility for much that is left entirely to the voluntary sector in India. Needs are less overwhelming in most areas, and the concentration of the church is thus on the spiritual side of life. Relatively few pastors see themselves as involved in changing aspects of society, as opposed to relieving need. So they do not feel bad if they are not changing society.

Having said that, we must add that society has changed in Britain. The socialist vision appears to have gone forever, and economic priorities have tilted further in favour of the haves, at the expense of the have-nots. The cold war has ended, but not the arms race, and devastating local wars have broken out even in Europe. Divorce figures are nearing 50 percent and most young people are living together before marriage. Religions other than Christianity are now strongly asserting their presence. Racism has been exposed as deeply institutional. The welfare state creaks and the social engagement of churches and other voluntary organizations is seen to be needed more than it has been for a long time.

The question we have been asking is how far a course in theological education enables students to confront these changes and how far they actually do so as they move into ministry. The same can be applied to changes in the church and religious context. The period we have surveyed saw the opening of ordination to the priesthood in the Church of England to women, a continuing decline in church attendance, particularly among youth, an almost complete ignorance of Christianity in a growing part of the population, a Decade of Evangelism in the 1990s that (many would say) did little more than raise morale in some quarters and perhaps slightly stem the rate of decline.

To what extent has the ministry of those from the West Midlands Ministerial Training Course stood up to this difficult context? Overall, the stories of the students we have looked at and others in the survey would suggest a fairly favourable response. The Course has given most students a flexibility that has enabled them to adjust as changes have come within and outside the church. Those from evangelical backgrounds have on the whole remained so, but rather than reverting to a backward-looking conservatism that has denied much of the experience of the Course, they have sat more easily within the diversity of the church. To be sure, in the case of some, the idea that mission is wider than evangelism has been a matter of lip service, but this may well be because of the environment within the parishes they have served. Others have enabled people to journey towards a more open and joyful evangelical faith and practice, embracing the bodies as well as the souls of the poor and excluded. On the whole, those who have come from the more liberal side of the spectrum have not become ultra-sceptical or secularist; and their training with evangelicals in the Course has probably been important in this. Mutual respect between "evangelicals" and "liberals" becomes part of a learning experience for both. Important also is the witness of the minority who have been able to remain as Ministers in Secular Employment. They can be in the forefront of the church's response to change in society, because they are more obviously part of it than those paid by – and therefore shielded by – the church. They spend their days with those who are often the victims of such changes.

Overall, however, the West Midlands Ministerial Training Course has been less successful in enabling its students to think structurally about the problems of society and to reflect on radical options for change. Its exposure programmes were less intense and life-transforming than those of TTS. Surely the part-time nature of the Course was part of the reason for this, but one must also take account of the more limited horizons within which a generally conservative church operates in the more comfortable West.

Both courses seem to have been quite successful in enabling students to continue to wish to learn. This is perhaps clearer in the West Midlands case, precisely because its part-time training is more limited and the range of available additional courses and further degrees is much greater. In the case of TTS, some have completed a two-year full-time master's degree programme, something relatively rare in England. But many graduates have taken no courses since leaving seminary, nor do they seem to have read very much. They are more ready to learn from life than from books.

By way of conclusion, perhaps each course should be judged by whether it is more likely to produce ministers determined to mould their own future and force it to their liking, or to produce people open to where God may lead them, in whatever experiences and within whatever changing contexts they are placed. Has it been an education that has impelled them, not only to good individual ministry, but also to facilitating others, so that the church can truly become the Body of Christ in the local context?

As far as the ordained ministry is concerned, a further test may be suggested by the ordinal of the church to which they are called. In the case of Anglicans, for example, has the course prepared them to perform various functions, sacramental and ministerial, but above all "to join the people in a common witness in the world", "to serve the congregation with joy, building them up in faith", that they "may be saved by Christ forever", and to be "messengers, watch persons and stewards of the Lord"?

The calling to a lifelong pilgrimage – of which the theological college or course is a part – has never been summarized better than in the words of the Covenant Service from the Methodist Service Book used in England and included in the prayer book of the Church of South India:

> I am no longer my own, but yours. Put me to what you will, rank me with whom you will; put me to doing, put me to suffering; let me be employed for you or laid aside for you, exalted for you or brought low for you; let me be full, let me be empty; let me have all things, let me have nothing; I freely and wholeheartedly yield all things to your pleasure.

A Short Bibliography on Theological Education

S. Amirtham and H.S. Cyris Moon, eds, *The Teaching of Ecumenics*, Geneva, WCC, 1987.

S. Amirtham, ed., *Stories Make People: Examples of Theological Work in Community*, Geneva, WCC, 1989.

S. Amirtham and Robin Pryor, eds, *Resources for Spiritual Formation in Theological Education*, Geneva, WCC, 1989.

S. Amirtham and C.R.W. David, eds, *Venturing into Life*, Madurai, TTS, 1990.

W. Ariarajah and S. Amirtham, eds, *Theological Formation in a Multi-faith Milieu*, Geneva, WCC, 1988.

C. Collier, *A New Teaching, A New Learning: A Guide to Teaching Theology*, TEF Guide (advanced) 25, London, SPCK, 1989.

K. Cracknell and C. Lamb, eds, *Theology on Full Alert*, London, BCC, 1986.

A. Gilmore, ed., *An International Directory of Theological Colleges*, London, SCM, and Geneva, WCC, 1997.

F. Ross Kinsler and James Emery, *Opting for Change: A Handbook on Evaluation and Planning for Theological Education by Extension*, Pasadena, William Carey Library, and Geneva, WCC, 1991.

F. Ross Kinsler, *Ministry by the People*, Geneva, WCC, and Maryknoll NY, Orbis, 1983.

H. Maybry, "Content Analysis of Theological Curricula", in *Religion and Society*, Bangalore, CISRS, Vol. 12, No. 3, Sept. 1985.

J.S. Pobee, Ofelia Ortega and Judo Poerwowidagdo, eds, *Towards Viable Theological Education*, Geneva, WCC, 1997.

G. Robinson, Henry Wilson and Christopher Duraisingh, eds, *Theological Education and Development*, Bangalore, Association of Theological Teachers in India, 1984.

I. Selvanayagam, ed., *Writing Theological Textbooks: Some Guidelines*, Bangalore, BTTBPSA/BTESSC, 1996.

James Francis and Leslie Francis, eds, *Tentmaking: Perspectives on Self-supporting Ministry*, Leominster, UK, Gracewing, 1997.

See also *Ministerial Formation*, the quarterly journal of the WCC on theological education; the journal of *ANITEPAM*, the association of theological education in Africa; *Chrism*, a quarterly newsletter among Ministers at Work and others concerned, published in Britain.